EXPLORING THE BIG WOODS

EXPLORING THE BIG WOODS

A Guide to the Last Great Forest of the Arkansas Delta

MATTHEW D. MORAN

The University of Arkansas Press
Fayetteville
2016

ISBN: 978-1-68226-010-4 (paper)

e-ISBN: 978-1-61075-594-8

20   19   18   17   16   5   4   3   2   1

Designed by Liz Lester

♾ The paper used in this publication meets the minimum requirements
of the American National Standard for Permanence of Paper
for Printed Library Materials Z39.48-1984.

Library of Congress Control Number: 2016936803

Here is your country.
Cherish these natural wonders. . . .

—THEODORE ROOSEVELT

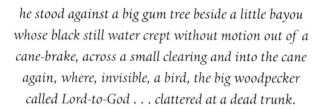

he stood against a big gum tree beside a little bayou
whose black still water crept without motion out of a
cane-brake, across a small clearing and into the cane
again, where, invisible, a bird, the big woodpecker
called Lord-to-God . . . clattered at a dead trunk.

—WILLIAM FAULKNER, *Go Down, Moses*

CONTENTS

Exploring the Big Woods

I still vividly remember my first time visiting the Big Woods. It was three days in January of 2004. I had heard about this place from nature enthusiasts, about the flocks of birds that crisscross the skies in winter, about the giant cypress that stand like sentinels in lonely swamps and bayous, and about a river that tumbles out of the Ozark hills onto an impossibly flat plain and meanders in its own lazy way down to the "Old Man," the great Mississippi River. I had heard that this was the last of the great Mississippi bottomland forests, once covering eight million acres in Arkansas alone, now reduced by 95 percent to a few remaining remnants, the rest ditched, drained, and cleared for agriculture where rice, corn, soybeans, and cotton are grown today on what might be the richest soil on the planet. I was told that I had better see the Big Woods now, for even this tiny museum-piece survivor might not persist in the face of the insatiable human appetites for resources.

My first day in the forest was one of constant sensory input. Birds in numbers too large to count chattered through the forest canopy and on the ground in their endless search for food. Woodpeckers hammered on trees in every direction. The smell of decay, not unpleasant at all, filled the air as the detritus from last season's growth recycled back into the ground. The White River, down because of the lack of rainfall in those far-away hills, still boiled and churned, its brown waters scratching at the land and the trees, trying to pull all things down with it on its long journey.

In my three days in the forest, I saw nature in its unencumbered exuberance. Big white-tailed deer bucks bounded off at the first sight of me. Flocks of blackbirds, some ten thousand strong, flew through the treetops, giving me a certain uncomfortable sense of nervousness. I saw more red-headed woodpeckers in one day than I had seen in my lifetime. Although all the animal sightings were exciting, what was most moving was the forest itself. Immense cypress, hickories, sweet gums, oaks, and sycamores stood guard over the forest as if they had been there for time eternal.

My second trip to the Big Woods was equally memorable. I arose at 2:00 a.m. to make the drive from Conway, Arkansas, down to the Big Woods to be there in time for sunrise. On this cold February morning, I crossed a small dry bayou into an open section of forest and sat against the trunk of a large oak, waiting for the first light to break. As it did, the forest came alive with the sounds of morning. Wood ducks swam by me in a nearby lake. Various birds flitted about the trees. A raccoon sauntered nearby and then froze when it caught my scent, quite surprised to see me sitting there motionless. An hour passed as the forest quieted down and the chill began to abate as the winter sun warmed the air. The long middle-of-the-night drive had taken its toll on me, and I drifted off to sleep. I was startled awake some time later, and at first I did not know why. As my eyes focused, I realized what had awakened me: a barred owl not twenty-five feet away on a branch, staring down at me. Our eyes met, and it silently flew off into the forest, landed about one hundred feet away, looked back once, took off again, and disappeared into the swamp. It was at that moment that I wondered how it took me so long to find this place. I knew then that I would be back often.

More people who are interested in nature need to visit the Big Woods. Perhaps in no other place in the mid South can you see wildlife at this level of abundance and experience a bottomland forest of this quality. Several endangered species along with many others in decline nationally, still thrive here. The White River and its tributaries, although partly altered, still meander relatively unimpeded through the heart of the Big Woods, periodically flooding the forest and releasing their supply of essential nutrients. There are few places in the Mississippi River Valley where this life-giving flood cycle persists. No less fascinating are the culture and people interwoven into this natural area. By exploring the Big Woods, you will learn much about the history of Arkansas, the westward expansion of this nation, and the complex relationship between humans and nature.

This guide is for those who want to visit this extraordinary place of nature. From 2011 to 2013, I spent many days exploring and scouting the locations described in this book. Over those years I came to realize how special the Big Woods is. The book is not exhaustive, but it tries to assist in your personal exploration of the Big Woods and begin your naturalist's education about this great place. The locations detailed in this book only scratch the surface of what is available. After you have sampled some of the locations, go out and find your own special places.

ACKNOWLEDGMENTS

Many thanks to those at the White River National Wildlife Refuge, especially Dennis Sharp (retired refuge manager), Ron Hollis, Marlon Mowdy, and Jay Hitchcock. The White River NWR provided housing for our many field trips, and the staff provided a wealth of information about the Big Woods.

The Arkansas Game and Fish Commission provided valuable information about its wildlife management areas. The Arkansas Chapter of the Nature Conservancy helped immensely for my planning of this project.

A special thanks goes out to Reggie and Mary Corbitt for their hospitality, information, and home-cooked meals. Gail Miller of Miller's Mud Shop provided great information on local food.

Hendrix College students were invaluable in assisting with the fieldwork necessary for this book. Special thanks go out Emily Deitchler, Dillon Blankenship, and Heather McPherson who made the time in the field so enjoyable and productive. Katie Kilpatrick helped construct the maps.

Charles Chappell, Professor Emeritus of the English department at Hendrix College read this manuscript for readability and grammar. Any mistakes that remain are products of the author and in no way reflect Dr. Chappell's impressive editing skills. Many thanks to my mom, Shirley Moran, who also pointed out numerous ways to improve the writing.

Randy and Judy Wilbourn, through their generous contributions to Hendrix College, made this project possible. Their long-time support of conservation in Arkansas has helped save the Big Woods for future generations. I could never fully express my gratitude for the work, generosity, and time they have dedicated over the years.

Special thanks to David Scott Cunningham, senior editor of the University of Arkansas Press for his enthusiasm for this project and Brian King, managing editor for making the final improvements on the book.

Many thanks to the love of my life, Jennifer Penner, who tolerated my long absences during holidays and vacation time so that I could explore the Big Woods, and then put up with me talking about it endlessly when I was home. I was always thinking of you when I was out there in the swamps.

INTRODUCTION TO THE BIG WOODS

*—the tall and endless wall of dense November woods
under the dissolving afternoon and the year's death,
somber, impenetrable. . . .*

—WILLIAM FAULKNER, *Go Down, Moses*

The Big Woods can be seen from space as a long, thin ribbon of green surrounded by the checkerboard pattern of farm fields in eastern Arkansas. The Big Woods is located in the Mississippi Alluvial Plain (often called the Mississippi Delta), the broad flat land that represents the region where the Mississippi River and its tributaries periodically flood and deposit large quantities of sediment. The region covers about 24 million acres of land from southern Illinois through parts of Tennessee, Missouri, Mississippi, Arkansas, and Louisiana before ending where the great river empties into the Gulf of Mexico. The region is characterized by a plain with almost no topographical relief, which is bisected by a complex of rivers, streams, bayous, and lakes, and is poorly drained. At the time of European settlement, almost the entire area was forested, and much of the area seasonally flooded (Nelson, 1997).

In Arkansas, the southwestern side of the Mississippi Alluvial Plain (fig. 1, Mississippi Alluvial Plain is in orange) is bounded by the West Gulf Coastal Plain, an area of low rolling hills covered by a mixture of pine and hardwood forests. To the northwest, the eastern edges of the Ozark Plateau and Ouachita Mountain regions form the boundary, roughly parallel to modern day US Highway 67. Within Arkansas, the Mississippi River forms the eastern boundary, although it is important to remember that small areas of Tennessee and a large area of western Mississippi belong to the same bioregion (Woods et al., 2004). A few unique landforms are present within the mostly flat Mississippi Alluvial Plain. Between the Arkansas and White Rivers sits the Grand Prairie Terrace, a slightly elevated landform that was once covered by extensive grasslands (Nelson, 1997). Running down the eastern edge of the state is Crowley's Ridge, a long narrow elevated landform with upland forest much more similar to biological communities in west-central Tennessee (Nelson, 1997).

The Big Woods today is just a small surviving piece of native veg-

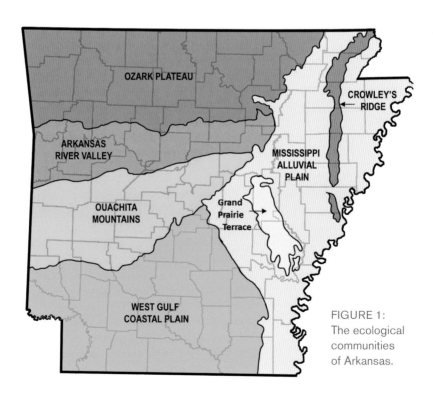

FIGURE 1: The ecological communities of Arkansas.

etation in a sea of farmland. The repeated flooding of the Mississippi River and its tributaries has laid down some of the richest soil in the world, so it is not surprising that the area became a prime agricultural region. Only in the lowest areas where flooding was most difficult to control did native vegetation survive, and today that is where conservation efforts are concentrated. That area includes the lower White River and a few of its tributaries, most notably the Cache River and Bayou DeView (fig. 2). The Big Woods also survives along the very last section of the Arkansas River where it joins the Mississippi River, although most

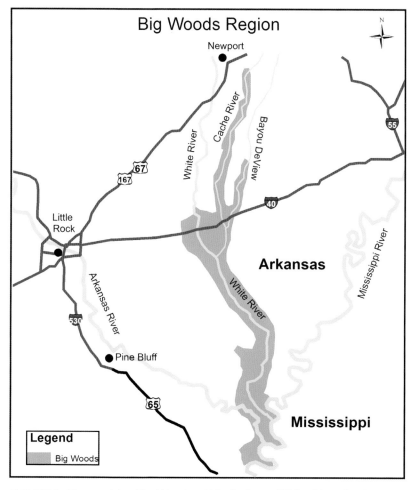

FIGURE 2: The surviving Big Woods within the lower White River, Cache River, and Bayou DeView region.

of this land is privately owned and managed more for timber production than for the benefit of wildlife.

The Big Woods of Arkansas almost disappeared forever because of the agricultural development of the nineteenth and twentieth centuries and the boom of river channelization and modification of the post–World War II era. If not for the foresight of concerned conservationists, it is unlikely that anything resembling a natural ecosystem would persist today. Fortunately, activities of federal and state agencies, along with the work of prominent members of Arkansas's hunting, fishing, wildlife, and recreational groups saved the last great pieces of this ecosystem. Today, there is the real chance that a portion will survive and even more parts will be restored to their former glory. Some of the animals are gone forever, but the forests and the floods that give the Big Woods life continue. It is my hope that we learn from our past mistakes and that this place can become a testament to our ability to save those things worth saving.

Hydrology

Four feet high and risin'

—JOHNNY CASH, "Five Feet High and Rising"

Water is the life force of the Big Woods. The reason the Big Woods still exists is the great fluctuation in water levels that occurs seasonally. While most of the Mississippi Alluvial Plain's hydrology has been greatly altered by river modification and levee construction, the area of the lower White River, along with some smaller tributaries, encompasses a region that still undergoes mostly natural hydrological cycles.

From July through October, when rainfall is relatively low and evaporation rates are high, water is typically found only in the main channels of the rivers and the many permanent lakes within the region (ASWCC, 1988). During particularly dry years, even lakes can dry out completely (fig. 3).

By November, rainfall tends to increase and fill depressions within the Big Woods in a process known as "puddling" (USFWS, 2012). These shallow flooded areas can expand over time if rainfall continues. With heavier or extended rainfall, streams and creeks rise and cause headwater flooding in the upper reaches of the Big Woods. These flooding events are often short term, but if rainfall continues and the larger rivers begin to rise (the Cache and White), they can spill over their banks into the forest. The flooding cycle is also affected by water levels of nearby rivers. Rises in the Mississippi River, often caused by rainfall and snowmelt hundreds or thousands of miles away, can block the flow of the White River. As the White River flows south and comes in contact with water backed up by the Mississippi, a process known as "backing and stacking" occurs, in which water levels slowly rise throughout the

FIGURE 3: Little White Lake, completely dry during a typical autumn period. White River NWR.

southern Big Woods (USFWS, 1994). Therefore, some years when the state of Arkansas is relatively dry, flooding will still occur because of the large geographic drainage area that affects the Mississippi River's flow. Backing and stacking can occur to a lesser extent where the Cache and White Rivers merge near Clarendon, Arkansas, as the Cache is frequently flooded by the White. This heavy flooding usually starts in December, and in particularly wet years almost the entire Big Woods region will flood. It is a spectacular sight to see mile after mile of flooded forest (fig. 4). The flooding usually peaks in February through April, after which water levels begin to recede toward their summer and autumn lows.

While the winter flood, summer low is the norm, the seasonal pattern is highly variable. Heavy rainfall any time of the year can cause headwater flooding that allows the rivers to rise and spill into the forest. Some years, low regional rainfall keeps the Big Woods flood free all year, or even for multiple years. Spring water levels are particularly

INTRODUCTION TO THE BIG WOODS

FIGURE 4: Flooded bottomland forest during a typical winter wet period. White River NWR near Tichnor.

difficult to predict since snowmelt and runoff from the Northern Plains and Rocky Mountains can send prodigious amounts of water down the Missouri River, into the Mississippi River, and cause flooding in the Big Woods. The large variation between years is vital for the ecological integrity of the Big Woods. Long dry periods can allow new trees to become established after sprouting, while floods of longer than normal duration can cause significant tree mortality. Some trees, such as bald cypress and tupelo, can reproduce well only during times of multiyear drought when their seedlings have time to grow above the flood water levels (USDA 1965). Some biological communities successfully reproduce only once every few decades, or even centuries.

These flooding cycles are incredibly important to the ecological health of the Big Woods. Tons of rich sediment eroded from higher elevations are deposited on the landscape as the waters recede. Thousands of years of these flooding cycles have created the amazingly rich soils that characterize the Mississippi Alluvial Plain (USFWS, 1994). The frequent flooding also provides access for many aquatic animals that would not normally be able to utilize the extensive bottomland forests. Numerous waterfowl, especially ducks, disperse into the flooded forests to feed on acorns and other nutritious resources (Delnicke and Reinecke, 1986). Fish spill from the major rivers into the smaller lakes and ponds and will even spend time feeding in the flooded forest. Flooding also selects for those plant species capable of withstanding inundation, while killing those plant species intolerant of such conditions, and is probably helpful in preventing the establishment of invasive exotic species (for example, water hyacinth, USFWS, 2012) that are such a problem in many other aquatic communities. For the human visitor, floods tend to clear out the understory of small plants, making hiking much easier during low-water periods. The depth of floods can also be incredibly variable, flooding the forest from a few inches deep to over twenty feet (fig. 5).

Alteration of the natural hydrological cycle by human activity is the biggest threat to the long-term survival of the Big Woods ecosystem. The major ways in which people have changed natural hydrological cycles are channelization, dam and levee construction, and to a lesser extent direct draws for irrigation. Rivers are often dredged, straightened, and their channels narrowed by wing-dam construction to facilitate ship navigation. This process produces unnaturally narrow river channels that increase water flow and drainage rates, which can in turn increase down cutting of banks and subsequent erosion. Dams modify water flows and can reduce the frequency of severe floods, but also prolong minor flooding by their slow water release over time. For instance, the dams on the upper portion of the White River (Bull Shoals, Norfork, and others) store water in the spring and slowly release it during the summer, at times flooding the bottomland forests for a time longer than they are naturally adapted to (USFWS, 2012). This summer flooding can be particularly harmful to bottomland trees, which although flood tolerant, require extended dry periods for proper root function.

FIGURE 5: Flood level indicator (20 feet) on a bald cypress tree. Trusten Holder WMA.

Levee building is the other major activity that changes water-flow patterns throughout the Big Woods. A large levee extends along a fifty-mile stretch of the eastern side of the lower White River, preventing flooding of the lowlands between the White and Mississippi Rivers (fig. 6). When flooding does occur, the water is forced into a much smaller area than it occupied historically, increasing water depth in the

FIGURE 6: Levee along the east bank of the lower White River.

forest and the intensity of flow in the main stem of the river. Areas outside of the levees never get flooded and cannot function as they once did. Levee building has no doubt made available millions of acres of land for agriculture and cities and has reduced property damage. But as the great Mississippi floods of 1993 show, levees can create a false sense of security and are not immune to failure (Larson, 1996). Trying to balance the needs of humans and natural systems is an ongoing process and one with which our society still struggles. The Big Woods, with its relatively mild levels of hydrological modification, represents one of the last places along the great Mississippi Valley where we can still view the natural flooding that once extended over the entire Mississippi Alluvial Plain. Only the decisions of human beings will allow that phenomenon to continue.

Plant Communities

The Big Woods is aptly named, as the trees reach impressive sizes. The long growing season, abundant water, and nutrient-rich soil assure rapid growth. Areas that were logged only fifty years ago look primeval again, a testament to the incredible growth that occurs in this habitat. In fact, very little old-growth forest remains today, since almost all of the Big Woods has been harvested for timber at least once. There are three basic types of forest present: bottomland forest, swamp forest, and upland forest, although ecologists have developed many subtypes within each major community (USFWS 2012).

The most common type of forest, the one that makes up about 80 percent of the Big Woods, is bottomland forest (fig. 7), which is formed in areas that are subject to periodic—typically yearly—flooding. That flooding deposits layers of rich sediment that continually replenishes the soil with nutrients and is the main reason why the Mississippi Alluvial Plain can become such good farmland when drained and cleared. There

FIGURE 7: Bottomland forest with a large overcup oak (*Quercus lyrata*). White River NWR near Ethel.

are several subtypes of bottomland forest, but various species of oaks (Genus *Quercus*) tend to dominate (USFWS, 2012).

Overcup oak (*Q. lyrata*) is the most common, easily identified by its distinctive acorn in which the cup almost entirely encloses the nut (fig. 8). Another important oak species includes Nuttall's oak (*Q. texana*), which although very common in the Big Woods, is globally restricted to the lower Mississippi Valley (fig. 9). Its acorns are important for many wildlife species. Water oak (*Q. nigra*, fig. 10), pin oak (*Q. palustris*), willow oak (*Q. phellos*, note the unusual narrow leaves, fig. 11), and cherrybark oak (*Q. pagoda*) are some other common oak species that are important for the ecology of the region. Associated with the oaks are several species of hickories, especially sweet pecan (*Carya illinoinensis*) and the most common hickory in the region, the water hickory (*C. aquatica,* also referred to as bitter pecan in many publications, fig. 12). Some bottomland forest communities are associated with large populations of sugarberry (*Celtis laevigata*), which is an important winter tree species for many berry-feeding birds (Kennedy, 2009; fig. 13). An additional major tree associated with the bottomland forests is sweet gum (*Liquidambar styraciflua*, fig. 14), a fast-growing tree that often colonizes recently disturbed areas. It tends to become hollow relatively

FIGURE 8: Overcup oak (*Quercus lyrata*) acorns on the forest floor. Courtesy of Leif Anderson.

easily and early in its life cycle and therefore provides shelter for many animals of the Big Woods. Bottomland forests also contain many vines, in particular muscadine (*Vitis rotundifolia*) and poison ivy (*Toxicodendron radicans*). High-quality bottomland forest is visible along most of the hiking and canoe trails described in this volume.

In areas of frequent and severe disturbance, such as lands near

FIGURE 9: Nuttall's oak (*Quercus texana*).

FIGURE 10: Water oak (*Quercus nigra*).

FIGURE 11: Willow oak (*Quercus phellos*).

rivers that experience flooding with a strong current, different bottomland forest communities are present. Some common species are black willow (*Salix nigra*), red maple (*Acer rubrum*), black gum (*Nyssa sylvatica*), and cottonwood (*Populus deltoides*). These river-side plant communities were probably once more common but today are rare because of modification of river flows. Large areas of this type of forest

FIGURE 12: Water hickory (*Carya aquatica*).

right, FIGURE 13:
Sugarberry (*Celtis
laevigata*).

FIGURE 14: Sweet gum (*Liquidambar styraciflua*).

now remain mostly in the lower parts of the Arkansas and White Rivers (fig. 15), and there are limited areas for good observation.

The second most common forest type is swamp forest (fig. 16), which is usually dominated by two tree species: bald cypress (*Taxodium distichum*) and water tupelo (*Nyssa aquatica*). The exact ratio of the two trees in any one area varies from pure stands of either species to almost equal numbers. These differences in relative abundance are probably the result of subtle variation in water depth and flooding cycles. Bald cypress is a spectacular species and the quintessential plant of the Big Woods (fig. 17). It is in the same family as the redwoods and sequoias, and although it does not reach the size of those two giants, it does share the family's trait of extraordinary age. Cypress can live for over one thousand years, and parts of the Big Woods contain stands of some of the oldest in the United States (Spond, 2007). An unusual feature of cypress is the "knees" that grow from the roots and protrude above the water's surface. The exact function of these structures has been the center of a great debate in science for many years. Originally it was hypothesized that these structures delivered oxygen to the roots, since swamp habitats tend to have soils with very low levels of this essential element. However, trees with the knees removed do not show a reduction in root oxygen levels. Other researchers have suggested the knees act as structural stabilizers in the muddy soil where cypress often grow (Briand 2000).

FIGURE 15: High disturbance forest along the White River. Wattensaw WMA.

FIGURE 16: Tupelo-cypress swamp forest. Black Swamp WMA.

Cypress wood is remarkably durable with a great ability to resist rotting. For this reason, it was and is highly valued, and most stands were cut for construction lumber many years ago. It is even possible to recover fallen cypress trees that became submerged in swamps many years ago and use them for wood today. A stand of old-growth cypress with their swollen bases protruding from the tea-brown water and their tops gnarled and twisted with extreme age forms a primeval picture.

FIGURE 17: Bald cypress (*Taxodium distichum*) and associated knees along the Cache River. Black Swamp WMA.

Good examples of swamp forest occur along all the major and minor river systems in the Big Woods, around most lakes, and sometimes in isolated pockets within bottomland forest. The best examples are found in the northern areas of the Big Woods, especially along Bayou DeView and in the Black Swamp Wildlife Management Area (WMA). Several of the best swamp forests can be seen along canoe trails described in this volume.

In areas that never flood, upland forest is found, most being along the western side of the Big Woods in a geological formation known as the Grand Prairie Terrace (fig. 1). This unusual landform contains a clay hardpan several feet below the surface that resists the colonization of trees and prevents rapid water drainage. Once covered in grassland and scattered forest and savannahs, most of the Grand Prairie is now dedicated to agriculture. Because of fire suppression, those areas not farmed are usually covered in scrubby forest composed of upland species of oaks such as white oak (*Quercus alba*, fig. 18) and post oak (*Q. stellata*), several hickories (*Carya* spp.), eastern red cedar (*Juniperus virginiana*), and various species of elm (*Ulmus* spp, USFWS 2012), along with dense grasslands on the forest floor (fig. 19). True prairie areas are dominated by big bluestem (*Andropogon gerardii*), little bluestem (*Schizachyrium scoparium*), and Indian grass (*Sorghastrum nutans*), and also contain many beautiful plants with showy flowers (fig. 20). Wattensaw Wildlife Managament Area has large areas of upland forest, and smaller areas of upland forest and prairies occur along the western edge of the White River National Wildlife Refuge (NWR). Just south of Wattensaw, a few small preserved areas of true prairie survive and are protected by state and private conservation groups (see "Sites Outside of the Big Woods"). The Grand Prairie Terrace was once inhabited by charismatic species more typical of the Great Plains such as the greater prairie chicken (*Tympanuchus cupido*), bison (*Bos bison*), elk (*Cervus canadensis*), and ornate box turtle (*Terrapene ornata*). Most are now extirpated from Arkansas, but a few smaller animal and plant prairie specialists survive today. Of the approximate 400,000 acres of prairie once found in this region, only 450 acres survives today (Arkansas Natural Heritage Commission, 2013).

FIGURE 18: White oak (*Quercus alba*).

FIGURE 19: Upland forest on the Grand Prairie Terrace. Wattensaw WMA.

FIGURE 20: Restored Prairie with tall specimens of Indian grass (*Sorghastrum nutans*).

Animals

"Hope" is the thing with feathers—

—EMILY DICKINSON, "Hope"

All the waters of the Big Woods drain into the Mississippi River. The Mississippi is the fourth-largest river in the world, both in length and drainage area (Biedenharn, et al., 2000, Kammerer, 1990). It is the largest temperate river system in the world. The river drains an immense portion of North America, about 1.25 million square miles, and all or parts of thirty-two states plus a small section of Canada. It is noted for its large array of tributaries, giving it a fanlike appearance across the center of the United States. Those numerous tributaries and their potential to create biological isolation have led to rapid evolution among many aquatic and at least some terrestrial groups of animals (a process known as allopatric speciation). The result is a highly diverse assemblage of organisms, the most diverse of those in any temperate river system. Mussels (Turgeon, 1988), fish (Bryant, 2010), turtles (Ernst et al., 1994), and crayfish (Taylor et al., 1996) are particularly diverse in the Mississippi drainage, including in the Big Woods. The highly productive lands within the drainage also support large populations of land animals. The lower Mississippi Valley in which the Big Woods is located is a particularly important area for migrating winter birds that find its ice-free habitats vitally important.

BIRDS

The Big Woods is a birding mecca with high diversity and often incredibly high densities of birds, especially during the winter migration period. The area is famous for its annual waterfowl migration, and it attracts duck hunters from around the nation. Besides the numerous ducks and geese, the Big Woods contains many other species for the naturalist's interest during this time. The summer migration should not be overlooked either, for although these birds are more difficult to see, they are abundant.

Winter Migrants

The Big Woods lies directly in the famed Mississippi Flyway, and every winter tens of millions of birds, primarily waterfowl and other aquatic birds, move from the Arctic, boreal forests, and northern prairies toward the southern United States in order to escape the cold and ice. Many of them settle in the Big Woods, sometimes in extraordinary concentrations. Although various aquatic birds can be found all year long, those residents are supplemented by incredibly numerous migrants in winter. Just watching the skies during the winter can be a great pastime as the flocks of ducks and geese move across the landscape and echoes of their "honks" and "quacks" fill the air. It is one of the great surviving natural spectacles left in North America and reminds us that although much has been lost, some great abundance still survives in our land.

Ducks (Family Anatidae) are by far the most numerous of the water-loving birds in the Big Woods, with approximately twenty species found in the area. The region hosts at least 10 million mallards (*Anas platyrhynchos*) each winter, the largest concentration in the world (USFWS, 2012, fig. 21). Many beautiful wood ducks (*Aix sponsa*) can also be found, some as resident breeders and many more as winter migrants (fig. 22). Massive numbers of geese, especially snow geese (*Chen caerulescens*) and, to a lesser extent, Canada geese (*Branta canadensis*) and white-fronted geese (*Anser albifrons*), can also be seen, although they mostly stick to fallow farm fields that surround the forested areas (fig. 23).

FIGURE 21: Mallards (*Anas platyrhynchos*). Courtesy of Matt Conner and the US Fish and Wildlife Service.

FIGURE 22: Male wood duck (*Aix sponsa*). Courtesy of Richard Hines.

FIGURE 23: Snow geese (*Chen caerulescens*) feeding on fallow farm fields near St. Charles.

Other water birds include a great many herons, egrets, bitterns, gulls, and numerous difficult-to-identify sandpipers. Great egrets (*Ardea alba*) are common breeding residents that can be seen in almost any body of water (fig. 24), as are great blue herons (*A. herodias*) and green herons (*Butorides virescens*, fig. 25). Common loons (*Gavia immer*), pied-billed grebes (*Podilymbus podiceps*), and American coots (*Fulica americana*) are common throughout rivers and lakes of the Big Woods during the winter. In the autumn, impressive flocks of American white pelicans (*Pelecanus erythrorhynchos*) follow the Arkansas River on their migration. Some will stay all winter, while others travel to the Gulf of Mexico. They can most easily be seen on sand bars of the larger rivers in the area, especially the lower Arkansas and White Rivers.

Very large mixed flocks of "blackbirds" can be found throughout the winter, both within the Big Woods, and also on the farm fields that surround the natural areas (fig. 26). It is common to find large numbers of red-winged blackbirds (*Agelaius phoeniceus*), common grackles

FIGURE 24: Great egrets (*Ardea alba*) roosting in cypress trees. White River NWR. Courtesy of Richard Hines and the US Fish and Wildlife Service.

FIGURE 25: Green heron (*Butorides virescens*).

(*Quiscalus quiscula*), Brewer's blackbirds (*Euphagus cyanocephalis*), and starlings (*Sturnus vulgaris*) foraging in noisy flocks. Some gather in groups of ten thousand or more. The rusty blackbird (*A. carolinus*), a species of concern that has declined precipitously in recent years (Birdlife International, 2012), can still be found in fairly large flocks, but almost always in wooded areas. The White River NWR is probably the best place in North America to see this increasingly rare species, where they can be found feeding on the ground, flipping over leaves looking for seeds and insects.

Do not overlook some of the smaller species that also winter in the Big Woods. Lots of small perching birds like chickadees, nuthatches, wrens, and sparrows will spend the winter months feeding in the Big Woods. In particular, large numbers of berry-feeding birds, such as American robins (*Turdus migratorius*) and cedar waxwings (*Bombycilla cedrorum*), can be found in locally high densities. Although there are plenty of resident woodpeckers and raptors during the nonwinter months, these are supplemented by many additional migrants in winter.

Woodpeckers

When one explores the Big Woods, often one of the first observations is the great amount of woodpecker activity. Their calls, distinctive hammering, and numerous tree holes are all testament to their abundance. Recent studies have indicated that the Big Woods may contain the highest density of woodpeckers in North America (Krementz and Lusier, 2010). You can easily see all seven species of common woodpeckers in Arkansas (hairy, *Picoides villosus*; downy, *P. pubescens*; red-bellied, *Melanerpes carolinus*; red-headed, *M. erythrocephalus*; yellow-bellied sapsucker, *Sphyrapicus varius*; northern flicker, *Colaptes auratus*; and pileated, *Dryocopus pileatus*) in a single day (at least in winter). An eighth species, the rare red-cockaded woodpecker (*P. borealis*, fig. 101), is found at a nearby outlying site (see "Sites Outside of the Big Woods"). For those wishing to view the charismatic pileated woodpecker, there is perhaps no better place in the United States to see it in large numbers. Winter is a particularly good time to view woodpeckers, as the resident population is supplemented by many migrants (especially red-headed and yellow-bellied sapsuckers), and the bare trees make viewing easier.

FIGURE 26: Mixed blackbirds flock feeding in fallow farm fields in Ethel.

Raptors

Raptors certainly find the Big Woods an attractive place, a fact which is not too surprising considering the number of prey available. With the banning of DDT in the 1970s and better legal protection in general, hawks, eagles, ospreys, owls, and falcons have steadily increased in numbers. While traveling down any highway, it is hard to miss the hawks, mostly red-tailed (*Buteo jamaicensis*), perched on fences and electrical wires. In winter it is not unusual to see at least one red-tailed hawk per linear mile of highway.

Other species of raptors are also common in the Big Woods, some as resident breeders, but many more as winter migrants. Red-shouldered hawks (*B. lineatus*) are common in the interior of wooded areas and will be seen on almost any trip. Harrier hawks (*Circus cyaneus*) are also common and are usually seen flying low over fields, with their white patch on the rump providing easy identification. Bald eagles (*Haliaeetus leucocephalus*) are now frequently seen, usually near water but also soaring over fields and forests. Several pairs of eagles now nest in the Big Woods, and the number of resident breeders is increasing (fig. 27). In winter, bald eagles can sometimes be observed attacking the large snow goose flocks in the area. Ospreys (*Pandion haliaetus*), once very rare in this part of the country, are now fairly common around major rivers and lakes. In the summer, large numbers of Mississippi kites (*Ictinia mississippiensis*) can be seen throughout the region, almost always on the wing hunting insects.

Four species of owls are present, with barred owls (*Strix varia*) being extraordinarily common. Almost any trip will produce a sighting, even in daytime, and any night spent camping will guarantee a visitor the opportunity to hear their calls echo through the woods (fig. 28). Great horned owls (*Bubo virginianus*, fig. 29) are also common, although they are less conspicuous and typically active only at night.

FIGURE 27: The bald eagle (*Haliaeetus leucocephalus*). Courtesy of the US Fish and Wildlife Service.

above right, FIGURE 28: Barred owl (*Strix varia*). Courtesy of Holly Bounds and the US Fish and Wildlife Service.

below right, FIGURE 29: Two juvenile great horned owls (*Bubo virginianus*).

Summer Migrants

When spring arrives, innumerable birds make the journey from Central America, South America, and the Caribbean to North America to spend the summer and raise their offspring. Although less well known or as obvious as the winter migration, the summer migration is equally impressive and involves close to one billion birds. Some of the birds that winter in the southern part of South America make a truly epic journey over five thousand miles. They spread out across the North American landscape, and some of them settle in the Big Woods, while others feed for a short time before continuing farther north. These birds begin arriving by late March and early April and will often stay until well into the fall. The wood warblers (Family Parulidae) make up a large portion of the summer migration populations. Sixteen species nest in or around the Big Woods, and many others migrate through the region during the spring on their way to more northern breeding grounds. Some especially attractive species that can be easily seen include the prothonotary warbler (*Protonotaria citrea*), which nests in tree cavities near water, and the hooded warbler (*Wilsonia citrine*), which can be seen moving through thickets and underbrush near the ground. Many species of warblers, however, nest high in the trees and are difficult to see. Two species of warbler that have declined precipitously can still be found in the Big Woods in relatively good numbers: Swainson's warbler (*Limnothlypis swainsonii*) in bamboo thickets, and the cerulean warbler (*Dendroica cerulean*, fig. 30) high in the bottomland forests along rivers and bayous. Both of these secretive species will require some careful looking to locate. Other Neotropical migrants include several species of flycatchers (Family Tyrannidae), vireos (Family Veroeonidae), tanagers (Family Thraupidae), and one species of hummingbird (Family Trochilidae).

Most of these summer migrants are small and can be difficult to detect, but the patient and determined naturalist will be able to spot many beautiful and interesting species. Early spring, April through May, when the birds are most active and before the stifling heat and insects of summer, is probably the best time to search for Neotropical migrants in the Big Woods.

FIGURE 30: Male cerulean warbler (*Setogphaga cerulean*). Courtesy of Than J. Boves, Arkansas State University.

Rarities

Occasionally, wood storks (*Mycteria americana*) and roseate spoonbills (*Platalea ajaja*) can be sighted in late summer, the northern limit of their range, although they do not breed in the region. Present on the sandbars of the Arkansas River are groups of least terns (*Sternula antillarum*), part of the endangered interior population. They should not be disturbed, especially during their summer breeding season when their vulnerable nests are being tended. You never know what other unusual bird you might find in the Big Woods as rare species are spotted almost every year.

The Ivory-billed Woodpecker?

To great fanfare, it was announced in 2005 that the ivory-billed woodpecker (*Campephilus principalis*) had been rediscovered in the Big Woods of Arkansas (Fitzpatrick et al., 2005). The paper, published by researchers from the Cornell Laboratory of Ornithology (plus several other scientists from other institutions) in the prestigious journal *Science*, reported several sightings of an ivory-billed woodpecker, possible acoustic evidence, and a short and grainy video. The news spread rapidly and was broadcast by many national news organizations. The sightings were concentrated within the northern section of the Big Woods, along Bayou DeView and within Dagmar WMA, two areas that contain some of the oldest forest. Local towns, such as Brinkley, attempted to capitalize on the discovery and attract tourists. It was without a doubt the most exciting announcement in the ornithological world for many years.

However, soon after the announcement, doubts began to emerge about the authenticity of the sightings. A long-term search was undertaken by the Cornell Laboratory of Ornithology in an attempt to document more fully the species and especially to capture indisputable evidence, such as a good photograph. Despite thousands of hours of searching over a five-year period, no solid evidence emerged, no nest holes were discovered, and no physical evidence was presented.

Further analysis of the video by several leading ornithologists concluded that the bird in question was probably a pileated woodpecker (Sibley et al., 2006; Collinson, 2007), a common and superficially similar bird found in the Big Woods. The Cornell team responded forcefully by saying that the data were being misinterpreted by outside authors. Some authors of the original paper stated that the ivory-billed woodpecker was extremely wary and secretive in an attempt to explain why no individual birds could be located. By 2009, Cornell suspended all searches for the ivory-billed woodpecker and declared the bird unrecoverable.

So the question remains, "Does this spectacular woodpecker exist?" Unfortunately, the answer is probably "No." When one analyzes the original paper, it is noteworthy that most of the "reliable" sightings were of birds in flight. Woodpeckers spend most of their time perched on trees, often remain relatively stationary, and are fairly easy to identify during such time. However, birds in flight are notoriously difficult to identify, and common pileated woodpeckers could be mistaken for the species in question if views were fleeting. Although some searchers have stated that the woodpeckers are extremely wary, that argument does not bear close scrutiny. Woodpeckers in general are loud, conspicuous birds that tend to be relatively easy to find. In the only detailed study of ivory-billed woodpeckers, which was done in the 1930s, Tanner (1942) found them to be relatively easy to approach, easy to locate once their home range was determined, and tolerant of human presence. Living *Campephilus* species in Central America are fairly easy to see and also tolerate human presence well (personal observation). As far as the acoustic evidence presented, the authors of the original paper were never able conclusively to eliminate the bluejay (*Cyanocitta cristata*), a notoriously accomplished vocalist, as the creators of the suspected calls. The "double rap" sounds heard could have easily been made by other woodpecker species while feeding. The most damning evidence (albeit negative evidence) though, was that searching for five years with literally thousands of person hours in the field could produce no solid evidence, only fleeting and unreliable glimpses.

It is of course impossible to prove something does not exist. But the evidence presented does not rise to the level of confidence. It would indeed be surprising that a large, conspicuous woodpecker could survive for over eighty years in an area frequented by hunters, fisherman, and nature enthusiasts, without producing solid evidence of its presence. Regardless, whether or not the bird exists does not detract from the natural wonders of the Big Woods.

REPTILES AND AMPHIBIANS

The Big Woods is a warm and wet place, so not surprisingly reptiles and amphibians abound. For those interested in these species, the warm months of the year provide a great opportunity to see numerous types.

Frogs and Salamanders

Amphibians, although present in large numbers, are not always easy to find. They tend to be secretive and are usually active at night. Frogs are the most common amphibians, with the tree frogs (Family Hylidae) being very common and diverse. Tree frogs are characterized by large toe pads that function as suction cups and allow them to climb effectively. They are usually explosive breeders, forming large congregations during the spring or early summer when they lay their eggs in temporary pools of water. Some species breed very early, often in February, including the spring peeper (*Pseudacris crucifer*, fig. 31) and the chorus frog (*P. nigrita*), whose high pitched calls are the first indications that spring is approaching. Others like the green treefrog (*Hyla cinerea*, fig. 32) and gray treefrog (*Hyla* spp., fig. 33) breed later in the year, often well into summer if weather conditions are favorable. Several species of ranids (Family Ranidae), including the familiar bullfrog (*Rana catesbeiana*), inhabit ponds and bayous and can be seen almost any place there is water.

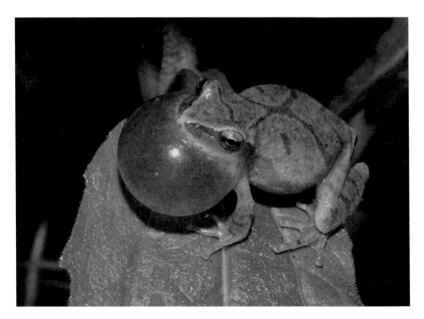

above,
FIGURE 31: Male
spring peeper
(*Pseudacris cruci-*
fer) vocalizing.

right, FIGURE 32:
Green tree frog
(*Hyla cinerea*).

FIGURE 33: Gray tree frog (*Hyla* sp.).

The Big Woods is not great salamander habitat since many species do not like frequently flooded terrain, as the Big Woods often is. Some of the few upland areas, especially along the Grand Prairie, actually have more species. One group that is found in abundance, although rarely seen, is the permanently aquatic salamanders. The unusual sirens, amphiumas, and mudpuppies are common in all aquatic habitats. They are secretive, usually very well hidden, and more likely to turn up on the end of a fisherman's hook than to be seen by the typical natural-history enthusiast.

Turtles

Reptiles are much easier to find than amphibians in the Big Woods. The southern Mississippi Valley is one of the regions in the United States with high diversity of reptiles (Hoekstra et al., 2010). This pattern is particularly true for turtles. The Mississippi River, with its numerous tributaries, is an ideal habitat for aquatic turtles (Bour, 2007). Most likely many species have evolved in the area and have also found a refuge here during recent glacial periods.

Almost any log, cypress knee, or other object protruding above the surface of the water can contain one or several turtles sunning themselves throughout much of the day. Sliders (Genus *Trachemys*, fig. 34), map turtles (Genus *Graptemys*), and others can be easily seen. They are hard to approach and will dive into the water at the slightest disturbance, so they should be viewed with binoculars if you want to identify them, which is difficult to do anyway. Other species seldom leave the water, including the softshell turtles (Genus *Apalone*) and the common snapping turtle (*Chelydra serpentine*, fig. 35). Neither of these groups should be handled as both can deliver a painful and dangerous bite. The softshells are particularly unusual in that they have extraordinarily long necks and can bite a finger placed almost anywhere on their bodies. The most impressive turtle is the alligator snapping turtle (*Macrochelys temminckii*), the largest freshwater turtle in the world, reaching weights of over two hundred pounds and living for over one hundred years. The feeding strategy of this turtle is unique. The tip of its tongue is modified into a fishing lure and imitates a small worm. The turtle sits on the bottom with its mouth open and wiggles the lure, hoping to attract small fish. When a fish approaches, the jaws are snapped shut with extraordinary speed, capturing the unwary victim. Because of overhunting and loss of habitat, alligator snapping turtles have become rare throughout their range and are fully protected in Arkansas. You are not likely to see one unless you find a female laying her eggs on land in the spring.

Lizards

Only nine species of lizards inhabit the Big Woods. About half of those are various species of skinks (the genera *Eumeces* and *Scincella*) which can be seen scurrying along the ground. One unusual lizard is the slender glass lizard (*Ophisaurus atenuatus*), a legless variety that spends almost all of its time underground. Lizards are more commonly seen on dry upland areas as opposed to often-flooded river plains. Some of the best places to see them are along the eastern side of the Grand Prairie Terrace that borders the Big Wood's western edge, in particular, Wattensaw WMA where the eastern fence lizard (*Sceloporus undulatus*) is commonly seen (fig. 36).

FIGURE 34: Young pond slider (*Trachemys scripta*). Courtesy of the US Fish and Wildlife Service.

FIGURE 35: Common snapping turtle (*Chelydra serpentina*). Courtesy of Matt Conner and the US Fish and Wildlife Service.

FIGURE 36: Eastern fence lizard (*Sceloporus undulatus*).

Snakes

Most people are not fond of snakes, but they are fascinating animals and important for the ecological health of biological systems. About thirty species are found in the Big Woods. The vast majority are the colubrids (Family Colubridae), a very large group of snakes that are not necessarily closely related taxonomically. All are nonvenomous or are mildly venomous rear-fanged species and no danger to people. Many *can* deliver a painful bite, however, and they often defend themselves quite vigorously. Most commonly seen are several species of water snakes (Genus *Nerodia*), usually found basking near water (fig. 37). They are often confused with the venomous cottonmouth (*Agkistrodon* spp., fig. 38), which they superficially resemble. Although not a threat to human health, they will bite vigorously if handled. On drier areas, rat snakes (*Elaphe* spp.), kingsnakes (*Lapropeltis* spp.), and a plethora of smaller species can be found.

There are five or six species of venomous snakes in the Big Woods. Many people have difficulty distinguishing venomous snakes from nonvenomous snakes, or they simply assume every snake they see is dangerous. All the venomous species of the Big Woods are pit vipers

FIGURE 37: A nonvenomous water snake (*Nerodia sp.*).

FIGURE 38: Cottonmouth (*Agkistrodon piscivorus*).

(Family Crotalidae). Pit vipers are noted for the pit organs, found just above the upper jaw, which are highly sophisticated heat-sensing organs (infrared-detection organ). This "sixth sense" allows the snakes to detect minute changes in the temperature of objects around them, an ability that is very useful in detecting mammalian prey (for example, rodents). A large heat signature can indicate a predator, so the pit organs also have a defensive function (Krochmal et al., 2007). All pit vipers have large triangle-shaped heads and rather stocky bodies, unlike most non-venomous snakes which tend to be long and thin. They also possess vertical pupils, like those of a cat, although you have to get rather close to them to see that trait. Pit vipers have modified salivary glands that are attached to two hollow teeth known as fangs. These teeth inject venom in order to assist in the capturing of prey and occasionally for defense. Pit viper toxin is hemolytic, meaning it destroys tissue, causing hemorrhages, a drop in blood pressure, and eventually death.

The number of deaths caused by pit vipers in Arkansas is extraordinarily low. Despite this fact, people often kill venomous snakes, or any snake, on sight. Ironically, many snake bites occur while someone is attempting to kill one. Snakes by their very nature avoid people, and if left alone will have no interest in a passing human. More importantly, snakes have important ecological functions. They prey upon a variety of small animals and help to control numbers of rodents, insects, and other creatures while in turn providing food for larger predators, especially birds of prey. It should be noted also that snakes are fully protected on public lands by Arkansas law, and it is therefore illegal to harm them.

Most common (and they are very abundant!) is the cottonmouth (*Agkistrodon piscivorus*), which can be found around almost any body of water (fig. 38). It feeds on fish, tadpoles, frogs, and other small aquatic animals. It has a reputation for aggression and can produce impressive displays. When disturbed, a cottonmouth will open its white mouth widely, revealing an impressive set of fangs. Typically a cottonmouth will also rattle its tail vigorously (but it does not have a rattle). Unlike the common water snakes (*Nerodia* spp.), cottonmouths do not usually flee. Cottonmouths also do not typically climb trees, which water snakes will readily do. So on the upside, if a snake falls out of a tree into your boat, it is almost certainly a nonvenomous water snake. Contrary to popular opinion, cottonmouths do not go out of their way to attack people, and they will readily go back to their own business after the person retreats.

Closely related to the cottonmouth is the southern copperhead (*A. contortrix*). Usually found some distance from water, they have extraordinary camouflage and are very difficult to see when concealed among dead leaves. Unlike the cottonmouth, they are very docile and will not strike unless repeatedly disturbed. Their venom is not particularly toxic, and there are no recorded fatalities from this species in Arkansas. In the mid South, the copperhead typically has a very beautiful color pattern. Copperheads feed on a variety of small animals, especially frogs and large insects.

Two species of rattlesnakes are found in the Big Woods, the timber rattler (*Crotalus horridus*) and the pygmy rattler (*Sistrurus miliarius*). The timber rattler is an impressive snake that reaches large size. Although potentially dangerous, timber rattlesnakes are fairly docile and do not normally rattle or become aggressive unless harassed. They are also reluctant to strike in defense and seem more content to use their very effective camouflage to avoid detection. However, if purposely disturbed, they are capable of delivering a highly venomous bite that is potentially fatal. The pygmy rattlesnake is a very small pit viper, which also uses its camouflage to avoid detection. With its small fangs, small amount of mild venom, and docile personality, it is not a serious threat to people.

Crocodilians

The largest reptile in Arkansas is the American alligator (*Alligator mississippiensis*, fig. 39). Once hunted nearly to extinction, it was one of the first species to gain full protection under the Endangered Species Act passed by Congress in 1973 (USFWS, 2008). From a low of fewer than one hundred thousand nationwide, the population has rebounded to 10 to 12 million. Alligators have been slowly recovering in Arkansas since they received full protection, but the Arkansas Game and Fish Commission has moved some from larger populations in southwest Arkansas to the Big Woods, where they had been driven to extinction. There is now a short hunting season for alligators on private land in Arkansas. However, alligators are fully protected on all public lands in the Big Woods.

FIGURE 39: American alligator (*Alligator mississippiensis*).

Alligators feed on almost anything that they can catch, including frogs, insects, birds, turtles, and mammals, although fish probably make up the largest portion of their diet. They are classic ambush predators, sitting motionless while waiting for something to pass nearby. They can also move with extraordinary speed for short distances. Alligators can be hard to spot at times as they often lie submerged with just their eyes poking above the water's surface. Many "logs" have turned out on closer inspection to be resting alligators. They grow quickly and can reach a length of fifteen feet and up to five hundred pounds, although it is rare to see one over ten feet long.

Alligators are now found throughout the Big Woods, although most of the habitat is not ideal for them. The frequent flooding means that alligators have a difficult time finding suitable nesting sites for their eggs and also cannot easily locate hibernation spots that will be free of water all winter. Basically, alligators need high-and-dry ground near water to reproduce and survive the winter. But they do wander widely, so you could see one almost anywhere in the Big Woods. The best place to see them consistently is in Arkansas Post National Memorial and some of the lakes in the southern reaches of the White River NWR.

Although large and potentially dangerous, alligators, like most animals, avoid people. Approach one sitting on the bank, and it will almost invariably slip into the water and disappear. They do sometimes kill and eat pets, so dogs should be kept out of alligator waters in the warmer months of the year.

MAMMALS

Close to sixty species of mammals inhabit the Big Woods region. Most mammals are nocturnal and therefore difficult to view, but they are often on the top of people's list of animals to see, especially the larger species. By quietly walking through the Big Woods, especially near dawn and dusk, you are likely to spot one occasionally.

Rodents make up a large portion of mammal diversity in almost all terrestrial ecosystems, and the Big Woods is no exception. Various species of mice and rats live in the area, mostly going about their business unseen by the casual visitor. They are important in dispersing the seeds of various plant species, and they are the food source for a many predatory birds and larger mammals.

The largest and most ecologically important rodent is the North American beaver (*Castor canadensis*, fig. 40). Outside of humans, no mammal has such profound effects on ecosystems. Their dam building and removal of trees can drastically change wetland structure and forest composition, and these actions indirectly affect the populations of many other species, some positively and some negatively (Wright et al., 2002; Rosell et al., 2005). They tend to increase the amount of permanent wetland area at the expense of seasonally flooded bottomland forests. There is much debate in biological circles about what the "proper" population size is for beavers. Bottomland forest with its huge production of fruit (acorns for example) is by far the most important habitat for many species, and beavers clearly have a negative impact on this forest type. Permanent wetland areas, which beavers increase, are also important for many species, although this forest type does not provide the abundance of food resources that bottomland forests do. It is also unknown how common beavers were before human settlement, although estimates range up to ten times current populations (Müller-Schwarze and Sun, 2003). They are quite well defended from most predators today, but in the past were probably preyed upon and their populations controlled by mountain lions (*Felis concolor*), which are now either locally extinct or exist only in very small populations in the Big Woods. Current management plans in most public lands are to limit beaver numbers through active management and the encouragement of hunting and trapping. Seeing beavers in the wild is easy by canoeing any of the waterways in the Big Woods, especially around dawn and dusk. Some beavers allow close approach, and watching their behaviors can be a fascinating experience. The beavers around Arkansas Post National Memorial, where hunting is prohibited, are particularly easy to observe.

The other rodents that are commonly seen are the squirrels (Family Scuiridae, fig. 41), of which three species are present. They are extremely important for seed dispersal of some trees since they cache many seeds each autumn. Although they retrieve these caches later for food, they often bury many more than they will ever eat, assuring that some will sprout into future generations of trees. Many oaks you see growing in the forest began life as an acorn buried by a squirrel.

The second most diverse group of mammals is the bats, with at

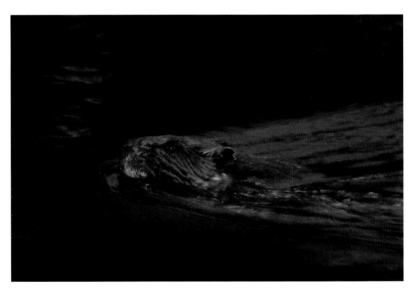

FIGURE 40: American beaver (*Castor canadensis*). Courtesy of Richard Hines and the US Fish and Wildlife Service.

FIGURE 41: Fox squirrel (*Sciurus niger*). Courtesy of Richard Hines and the US Fish and Wildlife Service.

least twelve species found in the Big Woods. Many can be seen flying at dusk, although identifying the exact species is very difficult in flight. The abundance of large hollow trees in the, especially sweet gum and bald cypress, provide numerous places for them to roost. Bats are extremely important ecologically as they consume large numbers of insects. All nonmigratory species are now threatened by an introduced fungus that attacks them while in winter hibernation. This fungus has caused dramatic bat declines in the eastern United States, and it appears destined to spread to Arkansas in the near future (Blehert et al., 2009).

Small carnivores (Order Carnivora) are relatively abundant in the Big Woods, including familiar species such as the raccoon (*Procyon lotor*, fig. 42), red fox (*Vulpes vulpes*), coyote (*Canis latrans*), and American mink (*Neovison vison*, fig. 43). River otters (*Lutra canadensis*) are common in major waterways and often can be seen foraging early in the morning. The bobcat (*Felis rufus*), our only common cat, is found throughout the Big Woods, but its secretive nature means that it is seldom seen, although spotting one along the roads at night is a fairly common occurrence.

FIGURE 42: Raccoon (*Procyon lotor*). Courtesy of Richard Hines and the US Fish and Wildlife Service.

Although possibly extinct in the Big Woods, persistent reports of mountain lions (*Felis concolor*) appear almost every year. Once common throughout Arkansas, mountain lions declined dramatically in the late-nineteenth and early-twentieth century because of overhunting and the decline of their major prey, white-tailed deer. As the deer have returned, reports of mountain lions have become more common, including some authenticated videos. Whether these are animals recolonizing from the western United States, or they represent escaped pets,

FIGURE 43: Young mink (*Neovison vison*) feeding on a rough green snake (*Opheodrys aestivus*). Courtesy of Richard Hines and the US Fish and Wildlife Service.

is a topic of great debate (Clark et al., 2002). Data support the notion that mountain lions are expanding in North America, and it seems possible that they could establish viable populations in Arkansas once again in the future.

The black bear (*Ursus americanus*) is a species that many naturalists would like to view, and they are now quite common in the Big Woods (fig. 44). Their history in Arkansas is no less interesting (Sutton, 1998). At the time of European settlement, the black bear was very common in Arkansas, to the point where the state became unofficially known as "The Bear State." French and Spanish settlers prized bears, not so much for their meat but for their oil. This "bear grease" could be used for lamp or cooking oil and was also popular as a hair gel. After the Civil War, bear hunting increased dramatically, and the export of bear oil became a profitable business. The town of Oil Trough in northeast Arkansas was supposedly named after the troughs used to store bear oil that was to be shipped down the White River during the late-nineteenth century. By the mid-twentieth century, bears were almost exterminated from

FIGURE 44: Black bear (*Ursa americana*). Photograph by Eric Dresser.

Arkansas, with only about fifty individuals living in the lower White River area of the Big Woods. The Arkansas Game and Fish Commission then began a remarkably successful restocking program, bringing surplus bears from Minnesota and stocking them in the Ozark and Ouachita Highlands. By the end of the twentieth century, bear populations had increased to about 3,500 in the mountainous regions of the state, while the Big Woods population had increased to about 500.

Scientists examining the genetic structure of bears in Arkansas have discovered that the black bears of the Big Woods represent a genetically distinct group, perhaps unique within North America (Csiki et al., 2003). They tend to be smaller than most other populations in the United States. Because of the large areas of cleared agricultural lands, the Big Woods population remains physically separated from the mountainous populations, which remain genetically like those found in the north. Now that we know they are genetically distinct, the conservation of the Big Woods population is even more important.

Big Woods bears, and those that live in bottomlands in general, have a particular problem during hibernation. Female bears give birth to their cubs while hibernating. In the Big Woods, winter flooding poses a particular risk to any mothers and cubs denning on the ground. Therefore, most dens are located high up in hollow trees, particularly large bald cypress, sycamore, and oaks (Oli et al., 1997).

Although you could spot a bear anywhere in the Big Woods, the best place to see bears is in the southern portion along the lower White River. The White River NWR from St. Charles south to the Arkansas Post Canal has good numbers of bears, as do the private lands along the Arkansas, White, and Mississippi confluence. Springtime, when females emerge from hibernation with their cubs, is probably the best time to see them. Males can be seen year-round, as they do not tend to hibernate this far south. Obviously, bears should be viewed with caution, but they tend to be very skittish in the Big Woods and will flee if they see or smell you.

The one surviving native ungulate (animals with hooves) of the Big Woods is the white-tailed deer (*Odocoileus virginianus*, fig. 45). Extremely abundant now, they were once reduced to only a few hundred individuals in all of Arkansas by the 1940s. Since then, intensive management by the Arkansas Game and Fish Commission has allowed them to thrive. Because of the abundant food supply, especially the massive acorn crops of the bottomland forests, white-tailed deer reach large size in the Big Woods. They can be seen practically anywhere, but are most common where forest and farmland meet.

There are several species of mammals that were native to the Big Woods and that are now missing. There is little chance for reestablishment, and they likely will be missing for the indefinite future. See the section entitled "Missing Biota" for more information on these lost species.

FIGURE 45: White-tailed deer (*Odocoileus virginianus*). Courtesy of Richard Hines and the US Fish and Wildlife Service.

FISH

You are not likely to see many fish unless you actually go fishing, but it is important to recognize the impressive fish diversity found in the Big Woods. The lakes, streams, and rivers are incredibly nutrient rich and productive, resulting in high fish densities. The varied habitat, from small ponds to large, slow-moving rivers, allows for high diversity. In addition, the lower Mississippi Valley is a center of temperate fish diversity, and many groups of fish evolved and diversified in this region (Smith et al., 2010). Several unusual evolutionary oddities, some very ancient, persist in the Big Woods as well, adding to this fascinating faunal assemblage.

About one hundred species of fish are known to inhabit the Big Woods, although the number is probably a bit higher considering the difficulty in sampling fish. The most diverse groups include the minnows (Family Cyprinidae), suckers (Family Catostomidae), sunfish (Family

Centrarchidae), and the perch (Family Percidae). Most well known and popular among fisherman are certainly the sunfish, which besides the fish referred to as "sunfish" by the general public, also include the black basses and the crappie. The largemouth bass (*Micropterus salmoides*), the most popular gamefish in the world, is one of the black basses, although most people do not realize it is simply the largest of the sunfish (fig. 46). It is an important top predator in freshwater fish communities. Crappie (Genus *Poxomis*) are represented by two species that are important intermediate-sized predators. The smaller sunfish, such as the bluegill (*Lepomis macrochirus*), red-eared sunfish (*L. microlophus*), green sunfish (*L. cyanellus*), and many others are incredibly numerous in the small lakes and rivers throughout the Big Woods and are also popular game-fish. The sunfish family contains twenty-seven species and appears to have evolved in the southeastern United States fairly recently, about 20 million years ago, and never dispersed out of North America (until recently assisted by humans). In most species, the males are brightly colored and in every case perform all parental duties. The males build a nest, care for the eggs, and guard the young fish larvae for some time until they disperse (Johnson and Gill, 1998).

Although not a large family in Arkansas, the catfish (Order Siluriformes) is well known to most Arkansans. About ten species inhabit the Big Woods, including several economically and ecologically important species. The blue catfish (*Ictalurus furcatus*) and flathead cat-fish (*Pylodictis olivaris*, fig. 47) are two large species capable of growing to over one hundred pounds and are some of the largest aquatic preda-tors in the Big Woods. The White and Cache Rivers are known to have good populations of these two large catfish, while the smaller channel catfish (*Ictalurus punctatus*) is also very numerous.

Several unusual species of fish survive in the Big Woods. The bow-fin (*Amia calva*) is the sole survivor of an ancient order of fish common during the Jurassic Period (201–145 million years ago), when dinosaurs roamed the Earth. The bowfin has several unusual characteristics, such as a primitive jaw structure and a lung that allows them to breathe air directly during time of low dissolved oxygen in the water (Nelson, 2006).

Another surviving ancient is the paddlefish (*Polyodon spathula*), which is fairly abundant in the larger rivers of the Big Woods, and can grow to over one hundred pounds. The fossil record of this group of

FIGURE 46: The author with a largemouth bass (*Micropterus salmoides*).

FIGURE 47: A flathead catfish (*Pylodictis olivaris*).

fish extends back over 300 million years. The long flat snout that gives the fish its name has numerous electroreceptors, which allow it to navigate turbid waters. It is a filter feeder, straining plankton from the water (Rosen and Hales, 1981). In most parts of its range, it has become rare because of overfishing and habitat destruction. The eggs of the females are highly sought as caviar, which are second in quality only to the eggs of sturgeon. Dam building has blocked its migration routes; however, the Big Woods region, especially near the confluence of the White, Arkansas, and Mississippi Rivers, still contains apparently healthy populations of this interesting species.

Gars make up a small part of the Big Woods fish diversity, only four species, but the spectacular alligator gar (*Atractosteus spatula*) is the largest freshwater fish in North America, easily topping two hundred pounds. This massive fish has spatula-shaped jaws with impressive rows of teeth. It can sometimes be seen resting at the surface, especially in the early morning as the sun warms the water. During the 1940s through the 1960s there was a successful sport-fishing industry in Arkansas that targeted these fish (Sutton, 2013). Unfortunately, catch-and-release ethics had not yet become popular, and the great fish were soon reduced to a fraction of their former population. Today, their population remains small, although they are still caught fairly frequently in the White and Arkansas Rivers, including some very large specimens (fig. 48). Contrary to popular opinion, they do not consume large numbers of popular game fish, such as largemouth bass and crappie, although they are very unselective in their feeding, easily taking turtles, birds, and small mammals if given the opportunity. Without stricter regulation, there is concern that this species could become extinct.

MOLLUSKS

The Mississippi River system contains an impressive collection of freshwater bivalve mollusks, commonly known as mussels. In fact, North America has the highest diversity of mussels of any place in the world, about three hundred species, with the upper Midwest as the center of diversity (Haag, 2012). The lower Mississippi Valley, including the rivers that drain the Big Woods, has many species, some unique to the area (Christian, 2005). Mussels are important to the ecology of rivers. Their

FIGURE 48: John Stortz with his Arkansas state record alligator gar (*Atractosteus spatula*, 240 pounds) caught in the White River in 2004. Courtesy of Richard Hines and the US Fish and Wildlife Service.

extensive beds can help stabilize sediment, and they filter vast quantities of suspended plankton from the water. Many animals feed on them including several commercially and recreationally important fish, such as the blue catfish (Eggleton and Schramm, 2004).

Freshwater mussels have a fascinating reproductive strategy. Since many live in rivers, they face an unusual challenge of dispersing their offspring upstream. Without a method to move against the current, they would, over the generations, slowly migrate downstream. They have solved this problem with an ingenious evolutionary solution. Sperm are released into the water and are taken in by the females to internally fertilize their eggs. There they develop into specialized larvae called glochidia. They are released into the water where they attach to fish, usually in the gills. There they remain as parasites (not causing much damage) for some time after which they drop off and settle in the bottom of the river. They are often released in the springtime when many fish are undergoing upstream migrations, and therefore they manage to disperse some distance away from the parent mussels, and often upriver. Some mussels even have specialized tissue that resembles a small fish and can be extruded outside the shell. Larger fish, in search of a meal, come to investigate, and the glochidia are forcefully ejected into the fish's mouth so that they can latch onto the gills (Haag, 2012).

Mussels also have an important place in human history. They were harvested by Native Americans for both food and material for tools. Later, a robust industry developed along the White River harvesting mussel shells for the production of buttons (Gordon and Harris, 1975). For many years, most buttons on clothing came from North American mussels. Plastic buttons replaced the traditional ones in the 1930s, although small-scale harvesting occurred throughout the rest of the twentieth century. The historical museum at St. Charles, Arkansas, has a good display explaining the mussel harvesting history of the region.

Unfortunately, mussels are some of the most threatened species in the world, and North America has already suffered numerous extinctions (Ricciardi and Rasmussen, 1999). The causes are varied, but the most important was the building of dams throughout the continent. Dams eliminated upstream river habitat and radically changed river conditions downstream. Pollution degraded water quality, and excessive sedimentation from land clearing smothered some species. More recently, introduced species, especially the zebra mussel (*Dreissena polymorpha*) from eastern Europe have overwhelmed the species that persist. Two endangered species, the pink mucket (*Lampsilis abrupta*) and the fat pocketbook (*Potamilus capax*) are still found in the main channel of the White River (USFWS, 2012). Numerous other species persist in the smaller bodies of water throughout the Big Woods, especially where water quality remains high.

Seeing mussels in their natural habitat is certainly difficult unless you are a diver. The murky waters of the Big Woods are not recommended for diving anyway, but many predators that feed on mussels often leave their shells on land where you can observe them. If you can find a spot where otters are active, you will often find the shells of several species, although it often takes a specialist to classify them.

ARTHROPODS

Insects, crustaceans, and other arthropods are abundant in the Big Woods as they are in most biological communities around the world. Incredibly important for ecosystem health, they inhabit practically every known habitat and pursue varied strategies for survival. Most arthropods have larval/nymph and adult stages that are quite different in terms of habitat use: that is, they occupy a different niche. Given their large abundance, it is no surprise that arthropods are important food sources for many other animals. The many herbivorous species also have profound effects on plants. In terms of diversity, no group of animals is even close to arthropods. Global estimates are difficult to make, but it appears that there are between five and ten million species of arthropods on Earth (Odegaard, 2000). In the Big Woods, there are tens of thousands and probably many that have never been described by science.

Crustaceans

Crustaceans are the most important aquatic arthropods and in the Big Woods are dominated by two types: crayfish and isopods. North America is the center of diversity for crayfish with over three hundred species, and Arkansas is well known for its high number of species (Reimer, 1963). Southwest Arkansas tends to have more species and several unique ones, but the Big Woods also contains an impressive assemblage. Besides the various bodies of water where one expects to find crayfish, they can also be found on land, usually areas with wet soils, especially the bottomland forest areas. Hollow mounds of mud (known as crayfish chimneys), sometimes up to two feet in height, show the location of their burrows, which often extend quite far into the ground (fig. 49). It may be tempting to try to dig some out for dinner, but it is exceedingly difficult. Crayfish are fed upon by a variety of animals, especially fish and small mammals. Two species of crayfish snake (*Regina* spp.) found in the Big Woods feed almost exclusively on crayfish.

Isopods are the other crustacean group common in freshwater habitats. Although most people are familiar with the terrestrial roly-polies found in the backyard, most species are aquatic. They are mostly scavengers and are important sources of food for many young fish.

FIGURE 49: Crayfish burrow within the bottomland forest. Courtesy of Leif Anderson.

Arachnids and related groups

The spiders (Order Araneae) are the most familiar arachnids and are found in almost every habitat on Earth. Although the web builders are the most well known, there are many other types, some that burrow, and others that prowl along the ground, or wait in ambush. There are even a few aquatic species. All are predacious and probably important for controlling other arthropod species. They in turn are fed upon by a wide variety of larger animals, especially birds. All spiders are venomous, but most are harmless to humans. Two species, however, are potentially dangerous: the black widow (*Latrodectus mactans*) and the brown recluse (*Loxosceles reclusa*). Both of these are common, even in houses, and their bites should be treated by a physician. Other arachnids found in the Big Woods include various species of daddy long-legs (Order Opiliones), one scorpion (Order Scorpionida), and ticks and mites (Order Acari). The most troublesome to humans are ticks, which besides being irritating can also carry pathogens such as the bacterium that causes Lyme disease. Most people know little of mites, but chiggers are familiar, small, almost microscopic ectoparasitic mites that can cause a severe skin reaction.

Insects

The insects dominate the world in terms of diversity, perhaps having more species than all other animals combined. They are numerous everywhere, and the Big Woods is no exception. The group is too large to cover extensively in this volume except with a brief overview. Although most people are not highly interested in insects, their observation can be quite fascinating. One of the best places to observe them is on flowering plants, where many species come to consume nectar and pollen. You can also search under or on the leaves of most plants and find interesting species feeding on plant material (fig. 50). One interesting feature of herbivorous insects is that many of them specialize only on one plant species, or on a small variety (Futuyma and Gould, 1979).

The one insect group that does attract a lot of attention from the general public is the butterflies and moths (Order Lepidoptera). Many are quite attractive with their bright colors and large wings. In the Big Woods, one of the best places to find butterflies as well as other

FIGURE 50: A northern walking stick (*Diapheromera femorata*).

FIGURE 51: Buttonbush (*Cephalanthus occidentalis*).

pollinating insects in on buttonbush (*Cephalanthus occidentalis*, fig. 51). This very common wetland shrub, usually found around the margins of lakes and streams, produces a round group of white flowers throughout the summer that attracts many species.

In the summer, the Big Woods often supports high densities of dragonflies. The extensive wetlands clearly provide a great breeding ground for their aquatic juveniles (known as nymphs), and the result is a sometimes extraordinary number seen flying throughout the region. Many species are very attractive (fig. 52)

The types of insect you will most certainly encounter in the Big Woods are the various types of biting flies (Order Diptera) including mosquitos, deer flies, horse flies, and gnats. Although they are bothersome, it should be noted that many of them are also important food sources for many larger animals.

FIGURE 52: A blue dasher dragonfly (*Pachydiplax longipennis*). Courtesy of Richard Hines and the US Fish and Wildlife Service.

Missing Biota

When I consider that the nobler animal have been
exterminated here—the cougar, the panther, lynx,
wolverine, wolf, bear, moose, dear, the beaver, the tur-
key and so forth and so forth, I cannot but feel as if I
lived in a tamed and, as it were, emasculated country.

—HENRY DAVID THOREAU, *The Journal, 1837–1861*

Like almost all places in North America, there are a variety of species missing from the Big Woods landscape, some extirpated from the region, others entirely extinct. The large so-called megafauna (literally, large animals) are the most obvious, but they are joined by birds, plants, fish, mussels, and other species that have been driven away by the activity of humans. Some were hunted to extinction, while others succumbed to habitat loss. It is only recently that humans have become concerned with the fate of species other than our own. In some cases, species that have been brought from the brink of extinction have either been allowed to recolonize or have been actively reintroduced back into their native range. The bald eagle, the American alligator, and the black bear are but a few animals now common in the Big Woods that were practically extinct just a few decades ago. Besides the moral and aesthetic questions of human-caused extinction, many species that are missing had profound ecological effects, so that their absences have significant detrimental effects on ecosystem function. Below I describe a few that were probably ecologically important for the Big Woods ecosystem.

CAROLINA PARAKEET

On the river lands, as usual, grows platanus or button-wood, upon the seeds of which flocks of screaming parrots were greedily feeding. . . .

—THOMAS NUTTALL, along the Mississippi River near present day Memphis, *A Journal of Travels into the Arkansas Territory during the Year 1819*

Most people today are unaware that the eastern United States once had its own native parrot, the Carolina parakeet (*Conuropsis carolinensis*). Once common in this region, they declined precipitously during the nineteenth century, the last one dying in the Cincinnati Zoo in 1918. Unrestricted hunting, habitat destruction, and perhaps introduced bird diseases led to their demise. They were quite common during European settlement times in Arkansas and until well after the Civil War. The bottomland forests of the Big Woods were a preferred habitat for the parrot and were probably their last stronghold in Arkansas. The last reports of them were from along the lower White River in the 1880s (Cokinos, 1990). What a sight it would be to see wild parrots living in the Big Woods today.

PASSENGER PIGEON

Pigeons—Warm weather has brot [sic] innumerable quantities of pigeons. The air is filled with them, and in the morning so densely that they darkened the sun.

—*Niles Republican*, April 29, 1843

It is incredible to think that what was once the most numerous bird in the world is now extinct. The passenger pigeon (*Ectopistes migratorius*) once formed unbelievably large flocks across the eastern half of the country. They followed the supply of acorns and other fruits and nested in colonies reaching up to one billion birds. Once they had consumed everything in one location, they moved on to new grounds, a giant mass of feathers moving across the temperate forests of North America.

Considering their population size, they were undoubtedly important for the ecology of these forests, consuming seeds, spreading nutrients, and providing food for innumerable predators. Their former abundance is clear from a look at the modern maps of the United States, which often include various Pigeon Mountains, Pigeon Hills, Pigeon Creeks, and so forth. Twenty-two geographic locations in Arkansas alone have names probably referring to this species (DeLorme Atlas and Gazetteer Series, 2011).

Unrestricted hunting during the 1800s and perhaps habitat loss led to their decline. Their colonial behavior during nesting made them easy targets for the market hunters that killed adults and chicks alike to sell in the growing eastern cities. By the 1880s, they were becoming harder to locate. Small flocks were seen periodically after that, but never enough to nest; apparently they needed the huge groups to stimulate breeding. The last one, Martha, died in the Cincinnati Zoo in 1917 (Cokinos, 2009).

Considering the immensity of their flocks, passenger pigeons would have undoubtedly had profound ecological effects (Ellsworth and McComb, 2003). They consumed huge quantities of acorns, hickory nuts, and other fruit. It has been suggested that the massive production of acorns by oaks in certain years, known as masting, is an adaptation to ensure that a few would survive the pigeon onslaught to sprout and become the next generation of trees (Kelly et al., 2008). Recent research has also suggested that the extinction of the passenger pigeon led to large increases in rodent populations (which also feed on acorns), increases in tick populations that feed on rodents, and subsequent increases in tick-borne diseases such as Lyme disease (Blockstein, 1998).

Today one can only imagine what it would be like to see a flock of over a billion birds. Although these birds are now lost to human memory, you can still ponder what some of the ancient trees of the Big Woods, still alive today, must have "felt" when the pigeons descended upon them.

RED WOLF

A wolf eats sheep but now and then;
Ten Thousands are devour'd by men.

—JOHN GAY, "The Shepherd's Dog and the Wolf," *Fables*

Wolves (*Canis lupus*) once ranged across all of continental America. Persecution by humans has reduced them to very small remnants of their original populations in the lower-forty-eight states, although they still are abundant in Canada and Alaska. The subspecies originally found in Arkansas and throughout the Southeast is the red wolf (*Canis lupus rufus*). Red wolves are smaller than their more commonly known gray wolves (*Canis lupus lupus*) of the northern United States and Canada. They are an apex predator feeding on small and large game, and probably important for the regulation of mammal populations. Driven to the brink of extinction by the 1970s, the survivors located along the Gulf Coast of Texas were removed from the wild and bred in captivity. They have been reintroduced to eastern North Carolina and a few select islands along the Gulf Coast (USFWS, 2007). There are no plans to reintroduce them to the Big Woods, and such a plan would undoubtedly face stiff public resistance.

UNGULATES

While the white-tailed deer survives today in great numbers, other hooved mammals once inhabited the Big Woods, notably the American bison (*Bos bison*) and the elk (*Cervus canadensis*). These two large mammals were common throughout Arkansas until the early 1800s. Bison in particular were commonly seen in the bamboo thickets along the Arkansas River during times of European settlement (Key, 2012). The Grand Prairie terrace with its extensive grassland also likely supported good populations of both bison and elk, although scientific observations were not made before their extirpation.

These two animals were quickly hunted out when Europeans began to settle along the Arkansas River and spread into the rest of Arkansas. There is little hope of bison being returned to the wildlands of Arkansas, but elk were reintroduced successfully in the early 1990s to the upper Buffalo River Valley in northern Arkansas and are commonly seen there today. There has been no study as to the feasibility of establishing a wild elk herd in the Big Woods, and it is unclear how well they would fare in the limited natural areas that remain.

GUIDE TO VISITING THE BIG WOODS

Timeless Morning on the Lake

When camping in the Big Woods, waking at first light is always natural. As the first rays of sun break in the east and the songbirds begin their morning chorus, and at the same time the creatures of the night—the crickets, frogs, and owls—go silent, a transition occurs that always startles my mind awake. It was one such time on a chilly October morning when I awoke to the sound of a cardinal calling vigorously in my camp. I arose and peeked out my tent into a windless atmosphere and gazed onto the lake only a few feet from my tent. Steam rose from the warm waters a few yards until it vanished into the air. One of the first big cold fronts of the year had just passed a day earlier, and the feeling of autumn was upon the forest. The cypress leaves were turning their brilliant rusty red color and would soon fall in to the tea-colored waters of the lake. A few Canada geese made their way to the south. Were they true northern migrants coming south to escape the bitter cold of the north, or just resident geese restless from the cold and the genetic memory of their migratory ancestors?

Today I was restless as well. The fall bite would surely

be happening, and I had my fly rod ready with the hopes of catching some crappie for the night's dinner. I hurriedly ate a snack bar, downed a glass of orange juice, and slid the canoe into the glassy waters of the lake. The canoe, my fishing rod, flies, and a cooler had all been prepared the previous evening so that there was nothing to do but jump in the canoe and go. I eyed a spot across the way that looked good, and silently (almost) paddled the canoe in that direction. Once in position I started the rhythmic, even artistic casting of the rod, two o'clock to ten o'clock, back and forth until the fly was at just the right distance to settle onto where I thought the crappie might be stalking a morning meal. Across the lake, threadfin shad flapped on the surface, and occasionally I could hear a larger splash. Maybe a gar, or a bass also eager for the meal, chasing baitfish to the surface. As the waters cooled this time of year all the fish in the lake would be eager to feed, I hoped, as they felt the urge to stock up before the long cold days of winter.

The process of the fly casting is almost hypnotic, beautiful maybe, and fully satisfying whether I catch a fish or not. Who could not help but be mesmerized by the almost weightless fly being zipped through the air in a big arching loop, then snapped back in the direction of a hoped-for fish, then slowing down in the air and falling, silently, onto the surface. I could almost be satisfied with just a bunch of well-placed and properly executed casts. Of course a fish wouldn't hurt either.

After about ten minutes I felt the unmistakable tug of a crappie, set the hook, and after a short struggle, had a nice one pounder sitting on ice in the cooler. That one was followed by another just a few minutes later, and I had enough for dinner. After a short lull, there was another bite, this one quite different though, and after a more significant struggle, a beautiful bluegill sunfish was held firmly in my hand. I am always impressed by how hard such a little fish could pull. The hook slid out easily and I dropped the fish back over the side of the boat. It darted off and disappeared in the brown water like a ghost. After that fish, it was a fruitless effort. Cast after cast enticed no more fish and soon I tired, even of the hypnotic flow of the fly rod. What short morning bite there had been evaporated, as it often does. A fisherman dreams of the never-ending bite, but those days are rare, if they ever happen at all. Also evaporated was the mist that had been just a few minutes ago rising off of the lake. The shad no longer slapped on the surface, and the predatory fish had decided to stay deep. Maybe they both had become fearful of larger predators that lurked above the water, like that great blue heron situated on the far bank. The soft light and vibrant sounds of first light had been replaced by the bright sun and mostly silent forest. A slight breeze had kicked up as well, putting ripples—imperfections actually—onto the once featureless surface of the waters. I looked up at the bright blue sky, brilliant no doubt, but it had none of the subtleties of a sky at first light. Magical moments come to the Big Woods often, but sometimes they are only moments. I paddled the canoe back toward my campsite and slid it onto the bank. I got out of the canoe, conscious of some aches that I had only recently developed, a reminder that time had taken a least a little toll on my body. However, I was content just to remember one perfect morning, now lost into the past, even if the very recent past. I hoped I could keep that moment in the mind, especially for those times when the Big Woods was far distant from my travels.

Orientation

SERVICES AND ACCESSIBILITY

The Big Woods is reasonably accessible for anyone with a vehicle. Rentals cars are available at the airports at Little Rock and Memphis. The more northern regions of the Big Woods tend to be easier to visit with abundant roads and a fair number of services. The southern areas are more remote with fewer roads and often limited services. To visit almost any area of the Big Woods, expect to travel over gravel roads. Most are of good quality and will be passable with any car, but care must be taken during times of inclement weather. Heavy rains and flooding damage roads frequently, so special care should be taken, especially during the spring and early summer when roads have been suffering through the winter weather. Some lesser-used roads are passable only by four-wheel drive, although all trailheads described in this book are accessible by a low-clearance car under dry conditions. Distances can be great when a traveler visits some parts of the Big Woods, so be sure to have adequate fuel before venturing far off the beaten path. Almost every small town has a gas station, although the cheapest prices will be found along Interstate 40. Keep in mind that cell-phone reception is spotty at best and definitely absent in more remote areas, so do not rely upon it for help.

One issue when traveling along the back roads of the Big Woods is the inconsistency of the road names and/or numbers. Published maps often differ as to the names or numbers of the roads, and often the actual road signs are different from all the publications. Sometimes there is no sign. I have attempted to list all possible names you could encounter and landmarks when necessary. For added assistance, I have provided latitude and longitude coordinates for all locations that can be difficult to find or are inadequately signed.

Hotels are available along Interstate 40, especially in Brinkley, which has the typical national chains. Smaller towns elsewhere may contain motels, but these are usually basic and not entirely modern. Since duck hunting is so popular in the region, there are several hunting lodges scattered throughout, some of which are spectacular structures. Most of the lodges also offer meals. However, these are designed primarily for hunters and are usually full during hunting seasons. Some are also open during the off-season. All require reservations, so always call or write in advance.

Primitive camping is allowed in some areas, most notably state wildlife management areas and the White River NWR. Most provide only a flat spot on which to pitch a tent. You will need to bring all supplies, including water. Private campgrounds around the Big Woods provide camping with more conveniences such as electricity, water, and perhaps supplies. As hunting is very popular in the area, most towns in the Big Woods region contain small stores that have basic outdoor supplies. Some truly fabulous small town diners and cafés are found in the region, offering some good hometown cooking with some of the friendliest people on the planet, and are especially rewarding after a long day in the field. I have tried to visit all the places providing services, but I am sure there are some that I missed. Please make it a point to visit some of them while in the area in order to help support the local economy. I have put an asterisk next to all establishments and attractions that are particularly rewarding to visit (see appendix 1).

To visit the Big Woods and see the really spectacular parts, you need a canoe, johnboat, kayak, or other small vessel (fig. 53). Unfortunately, there are few canoe rentals in the area, although some establishments do rent flat-bottomed johnboats. Several companies offer guided nature tours outside of duck-hunting season, and they typically provide everything you need for a trip. See appendix 1 for information about lodging, supplies, and local attractions at the various communities within and around the Big Woods.

DANGERS AND ANNOYANCES

The Big Woods is not without its dangers. The major killers in most outdoor situations are hypothermia (exposure) or drowning, and the Big Woods is no different. First and foremost, always wear a flotation device

FIGURE 53: Paddling in the Big Woods on H-Lake. White River NWR.
Courtesy of Dillon Blankenship.

while boating. It does not matter how good a swimmer you are. It is
easy to get injured if a boat overturns. Injury often leads to panic, which
can quickly cause drowning. Every year several people die in Arkansas
boating accidents who would have survived if they had been wearing a
flotation device. All vessels are required by law to contain one flotation
device per person when in operation. If boating in the colder months of
the year, staying warm is of primary importance. Overturning in cold
water can quickly lead to hypothermia and death. As little as twenty
minutes in water below 40°F can be fatal, and any temperature below
70°F can eventually cause hypothermia. Unfortunately, the victim may
not recognize the symptoms, and as body temperatures drops, confu-
sion, poor decision-making, and lethargy can result. When it is cold, I
always travel with a dry bag that contains a towel, a change of clothes,
waterproof matches, and some food and water. Those few items could

save your life. It is also advisable to check the weather carefully. Mild winter days can turn bitterly cold and windy when a frontal system approaches.

The waters of the Big Woods harbor strong currents that can also be dangerous. One look at the White or Arkansas River, and it is obvious that these two should not be treated lightly. Even in low water they can be surprisingly swift, while in high water they can be downright treacherous. Smaller rivers and streams can also be dangerous during high water or during floods. During flood conditions, you can often float through the bottomland forests where there is little or no current. However, be cautious not to paddle mistakenly into a chute or creek where the current could suddenly be quite swift. If you arrive at a launching point and the river looks too swift, do not proceed. Consulting with locals or with state or federal offices of the wildlife areas can also help. Above all, use common sense. Keep in mind that many areas are very remote, and help is unlikely to arrive in a short period of time. You must plan on being self-sufficient.

The summer months with high temperatures and humidity provide the environment in which heat exhaustion or heat stroke can occur. If exercising vigorously in hot weather, be aware that this medical condition can develop rapidly. By limiting activity to the early morning and late afternoons, the risk is diminished.

One final note on boating. If a thunderstorm approaches, get off the water immediately. Lightning is a particularly dangerous killer, especially for someone in an exposed boat. Stop all boating activities when lightning is visible or thunder is audible. Thunderstorms can develop quickly and unpredictably in Arkansas, especially in the spring and summer, and can be particularly violent.

The Big Woods has its share of hazardous animals, although their dangers are almost always overblown. Venomous snakes include the cottonmouth, copperhead, and two species of rattlesnakes. You will almost certainly see cottonmouths during the warmer times of the year. All snakes want to avoid you, so by giving them some room they will leave you alone as well. If bitten by one of these snakes, seek medical advice and remember that a fatality is extremely unlikely. Bites are extremely rare anyway. In my twenty-five–plus years in wild areas, I have never been bitten by a venomous snake, although I have seen plenty. Wearing sturdy shoes that provide good ankle protection is the best way to avoid a bite in case you do step on a venomous snake. Leave the flip-flops at home!

Although uncommon, alligators are found in the Big Woods and are a potential risk. Once again, by keeping your distance when you spot one, you will avoid any problems. Do be especially careful with pets where alligators are present since they will sometimes view a dog or cat as a potential meal. Wild hogs (*Sus scrofa*) have been introduced into the Big Woods region. Their ferocity is overrated, but they are quite capable of defending themselves with their sheer bulk and sharp tusks. They travel in herds and should not be harassed, as the large males can be aggressive when defending their group. Finally, there are bears in the Big Woods. Individuals of this population tend to be extremely wary of people though, and it is very hard to see one even if you are trying. They will almost always flee at the first sign of a person. However, when camping, please keep food locked in your vehicle or in another inaccessible location. As the saying goes, "a fed bear is a dead bear," and habituated bears usually have to be destroyed as they lose their fear of humans or associate people with food.

There are plenty of biting insects in the Big Woods, especially during the warmer months of the year. Mosquitoes, black flies, deer flies, and others can harass a visitor, sometimes severely. The number of biting insects can vary dramatically and is probably dependent upon complex patterns of rainfall and temperatures. It is very difficult to predict how bad they will be on a given day. I have visited during the heat of summer and encountered almost no biting insects and have experienced them so bad in November that I had to leave. Insect repellent will certainly help with the mosquitoes, although its effectiveness for other insects in questionable. Fortunately, ticks and chiggers are relatively uncommon in the Big Woods, at least compared to other parts of Arkansas where their numbers are legendary. Presumably the frequent flooding kills them off yearly and, therefore, prevents their populations from expanding. One exception is the upland areas that do not flood (e.g. Wattensaw WMA), which can contain ticks and chiggers in abundance.

One should not forget about the plants. The only one to worry about seriously is poison ivy (*Toxicodendron radicans*), which is quite common throughout the area. It grows as a thick hairy vine up the sides of trees and also spreads along the ground from underground stems (fig. 54). Learn to recognize it, as many people develop dermatitis if they come in direct contact. All parts of the plant contain the toxin urushiol, which irritates the skin. Also be careful if building a fire since inhaling the smoke from poison ivy can cause serious damage to the lungs. A few other plants, such as honey locust (*Gleditsia triacanthos*) and devil's walking stick (*Aralia spinosa*) have impressive spines that can cause a painful experience, but are no serious threat.

As noted before, hunting is popular throughout the Big Woods, and almost all areas described in the book allow hunting, including hunting for deer. During deer season, it is important to wear hunter orange at all times while in the woods. Camping sites also can become scarce during deer season. Many of the hunters in the Big Woods are local and quite familiar with the region. Strike up a conversation, and they might point you toward excellent places to explore. The Arkansas Game and Fish Commission website contains hunting-season information. Federal lands usually have more restrictive hunting regulations when compared to state rules, and they also post these on their individual websites. For safety reasons, some areas are closed to nonhunters during modern gun seasons. Please review current regulations before venturing into the Big Woods.

FOR THOSE UNFAMILIAR WITH VISITING THE BOTTOMLANDS

For first time visitors, exploring the bottomlands of eastern Arkansas can seem daunting. The flat and seemingly featureless landscape can at first appear difficult to navigate. It is true that landmarks can be hard to find as you pass by endless, similar looking stands of trees. The rise and fall of water during the seasons also changes where and how you can go through these woods. Also, some people are just frightened by the notion of entering swamps.

Be assured though that exploring these lands should generate no more trepidation than any other wild place in Arkansas. Bodies of water, such as lakes, bayous, and chutes, provide valuable landmarks. They also make the best travel routes. Trees are not all the same. Some cypress, tupelo, and sycamore take on bizarre shapes and can be useful

FIGURE 54: Poison ivy (*Toxicodendron radi-cans*). a) the leaves and b) the vines.

landmarks when traversing unfamiliar territory. Take time to examine the trees and look for the subtle cues that distinguish them as individuals.

The water, and in particular its rise and fall of the floods, can cause significant trepidation to the novice visitor as well. For one, the dry land looks completely different when covered by a layer of water. My recommendation is to travel close to established routes during the flood unless you are experienced in the Big Woods. Nonetheless, everyone should at least spend some time traveling through the flooded forest. It is a spectacular experience.

INDISPENSABLE RESOURCES

The locations of every trail described in this book can be found on either figure 55 or 74. Every visitor to the Big Woods will want to carry a few published resources besides this book to assist exploration. The *Arkansas Atlas and Gazetteer* (DeLorme Atlas and Gazetteer Series, 2011) is invaluable for finding your way around the back roads of the Big Woods, but remember that road names and / or numbers are not always correct compared to what is posted in the field. For those who want extremely detailed maps, the White River NWR sells topographical maps of their refuge, as well as those for the Cache River NWR. State wildlife management area maps can be downloaded from the Internet (see appendix 2). For historical purposes, Thomas Nuttall's *A Journal of Travels into the Arkansas Territory during the Year 1819* (Nuttall, 1819) makes a fascinating read for anyone interested in the early European settlement of the region. Some of his observations of the plants and animals of the Big Woods are illuminating about how the natural environment once appeared. Tim Ernst publishes several excellent hiking guides to Arkansas, and his *Arkansas Nature Lover's Guidebook* (Ernst, 2006) has a good section on the Big Woods. Recommended field guides include *Wildflowers of Arkansas* (Hunter, 2000), *Trees, Shrubs, and Vines of Arkansas* (Hunter, 2000), *The Sibley Guide to Birds* (Sibley, 2000), and *The Peterson Field Guide to Reptiles and Amphibians: Eastern and Central North America* (Collins et al., 1998).

TOP FIVE TRIPS

If you have the opportunity to visit the Big Woods for only a short period of time, here is a list of the five best destinations. Detailed descriptions of each are found on later pages of this book.

1. Bayou DeView Swamp Canoe Trail
2. Cache River Canoe Trail
3. Big Cypress Tree Trail
4. East Moon Lake / Parish Lakes Float
5. Robe Bayou Canoe Trail

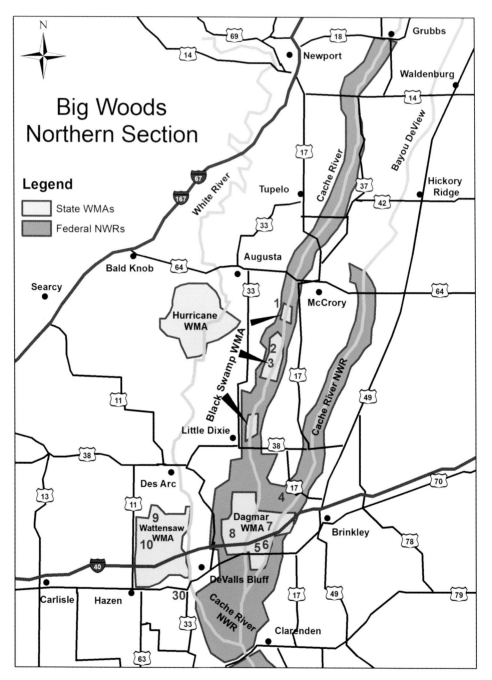

FIGURE 55: Map of the northern Big Woods region with public lands and major roads and towns. Numbers in red indicate location of described trails.

Northern Big Woods

The northern portion of the Big Woods extends from Route 18 in the vicinity of Newport to Route 79 at Clarendon (fig. 55). Most of this region is highly fragmented with forested areas isolated in a sea of farmland. It is quite accessible with many good roads and boat ramps. Much of the conservation effort by various private groups and public-conservation departments has focused on reconnecting the isolated areas by creating reforested corridors. Although this area has undergone the greatest human impact, it also contains some of the most spectacular forest in the Big Woods, and almost all the unharvested old-growth swamp forests that survive are found here. Since it is fairly far upstream, the northern Big Woods tends to remain flooded for shorter periods of time, and only after heavy rains. Water flows through this region rapidly, and rises in the Mississippi River do not normally have an effect. Many times when the lower White River has flooded all the land around it, the northern Big Woods is still dry and easy to explore.

Most of the public land is within the Cache River NWR, but much of it is fragmented and interspersed with private land, and therefore has limited access. Three important state management areas are Dagmar, Wattensaw, and the Black Swamp, which have excellent access and some of the best Big Woods habitat. The Hurricane WMA is an isolated piece of forest that has many Big Woods characteristics but is not included in this book.

CACHE RIVER NATIONAL WILDLIFE REFUGE: US FISH AND WILDLIFE SERVICE

It was a monumental fight to save the Cache River, but the dispute was ultimately settled by the creation of the Cache River NWR in 1986. The refuge protects the lower portions of the Cache River from Newport to Clarendon where the Cache joins the White River, and much of Bayou DeView (fig. 55). Two important state management areas are interspersed within the refuge, Dagmar and the Black Swamp WMAs. While Dagmar is a large contiguous state-managed area, the Black Swamp is composed of several small inholdings within the Cache River NWR. The refuge is still in the land-acquisition phase, so there are numerous, often scattered public-land holdings, sometimes surrounded by private land. Currently, about 68,000 acres is owned by the refuge, about half of the eventual goal. One of the important charges of the Cache River NWR is to replant bottomland forests. While traveling around the refuge, you will often see the results of these reforestation efforts in fields covered with small native trees. One day these will grow into impressive stands, provide ideal wildlife habitat, and help extend an important migration corridor for the Big Woods. Visitor services are limited, and access is primarily by water. You may not cross private land to reach refuge land without landowner permission. However, all navigable waters are public, including all of the Cache River and Bayou DeView. The main office is located in a small facility at Little Dixie, on Route 33, about sixteen miles south of Augusta, and it has detailed maps of the refuge.

The Cache River has many access points where you can float. Two sections are described in detail below, and several others are described briefly. Theoretically, the Cache River can be floated along almost its entire length. But between the Black Swamp WMA and US Highway Route 70, a very long distance, there is no reliable boat launch. The sections of the book describing Black Swamp and Dagmar WMAs in detail also include parts of the Cache River NWR. The Cache River NWR is closed to nonhunters during the annual deer quota hunt and certain areas are closed during the winter duck migration. Be sure to check their website (appendix 2) for current regulations before visiting the refuge.

DISTANCE: 9.1 miles
TIME: 6 hours
DIFFICULTY: moderate

DIRECTIONS: The float starts at the Highway 260 crossing of the Cache River (35.225543 N, 91.253950 W). From Augusta, travel 1.0 mile on Route 64, and turn right (south) onto Route 33. Travel for 3.0 miles and turn left onto Route 260. Travel 5.2 miles, and a sign will indicate the boat launch. Turn right just before the river and then make an immediate left. The road ends at the boat launch. To reach the launch for the end of the float, follow Route 33 south from just east of Augusta for 9.1 miles to Gregory. Turn left onto County Road 752 (1st Street in the town of Gregory) where a sign indicates the Rex Hancock Black Swamp WMA. Follow the road for 1.5 miles and turn right onto County Road 745, where another sign marks the refuge entrance (Rex Hancock Road or Railroad Dump Access, depending on which map you are following). Follow the road 1.6 miles to its end where the launch is located (35.151897 N, 91.288389 W).

FIGURE 56: Cache River near Augusta. Cache River NWR.

This beautiful float travels down the middle portion of the Cache River (fig. 56) and is particularly good for viewing wildlife. This is one of my favorite floats in the Big Woods. A diversity of habitats will be encountered along the float, including high-quality tupelo/cypress swamp, bottomland forests, willow thickets, and small lakes. A few old-growth stands of forest are found along the route as well. Wildlife seems particularly abundant. During the warmer times of the year, you will see large numbers of nesting wood ducks, small mammals, and many reptiles. Cottonmouths and a variety of nonvenomous water snakes are common. The attractive and harmless banded water snake (*Nerodia fasciata*) seems particularly abundant. The float is moderately challenging, and the last 5.0 miles traverse a fairly narrow, winding channel with numerous overhanging branches, and sometimes debris that will require a portage. Before attempting this trip, you should have basic canoeing skills and experience. The float can be difficult in low water and dangerous in high water. Call the Cache River Refuge at 870-347-2614 for current conditions. It should also be noted that fisherman hang limb lines on many of the trees to catch catfish, so be careful when passing under overhanging branches.

The float begins in an open water area at the Route 260 launch (fig. 57). The first couple of miles are open water. Most of the land along the river is high-quality bottomland forest, although mostly young, and there is a thin line of cypress and tupelo along the margin of the river. At mile 1.9 you reach the first narrow section of the river, and there are two possible pathways as the river splits. The left route is shorter, although the right route appears a bit deeper. Each is passable. At mile 2.4, the two branches rejoin and enter another open-water area similar to the first section. The relatively open area continues for 1.2 miles to a sharp bend in the river and an apparent split. To the right is Penn Bay (35.198183 N, 91.269260 W), which is a picturesque side lake attached to the main river. Please note that all the land around the bay is private, so while you can paddle into the bay, no landing is allowed. To the left, the river continues downstream passing through more high-quality bottomland forest.

At mile 5.3 the river changes character dramatically and enters the northern part of the Black Swamp (35.177395 N, 91.276259 W). Here the river is narrow, winding, and highly braided. Exactly which branch to take is not always clear, but by following the strongest water current, the route will be fairly obvious. The river now passes through very nice swamp forest of tupelo and cypress while red maple and black willow often line the very edge of the river. Most of it was harvested in the past, but there are still a few areas that exhibit old-growth characteristics. There are probably some cypress in the eight-hundred-year-old range, and some equally impressive tupelo with grotesquely swollen bases. Wildlife viewing is particularly good through this region, and you can often come around a bend in the river and be suddenly close to animals. There are plenty of snags and stumps in the main channel, and you can expect a few portages along the way where trees have fallen across the river, although none are particularly difficult. Most of the land along the Black Swamp stretch is public, either the Cache River NWR or the Black Swamp WMA, so you can get out of the canoe any time and explore the forest if the water is low. However the swamp makes for tough travel, and you are unlikely to get very far before finding deep mud.

This swamp continues for 3.0 miles with only an occasional open water area. The exact route is not always obvious, but if you simply follow the current, you will end up at your destination. At mile 8.4, a private landholding that is well marked will appear on the east bank (left) of the river, indicating that you are nearing the end of your journey. At mile 8.8, the narrow and winding river abruptly ends at what appears to be a T junction. To the right is a short bay, while the river continues to the left. Paddle a short distance to mile 8.9, and the boat launch will appear at the end of a channel (35.151553 N, 91.285150 W). Although the human-made channel is obvious, it is not necessarily marked well, so be careful not to pass it. Paddle the last 0.2 miles to reach the boat launch.

Other Cache River Float Trips

With many access points and good scenery throughout, much of the Cache River makes for great floats. Most of the waterway is managed by the Cache River NWR, but there is much private land surrounding the river. Please do not leave the river unless you are sure the land is public. The Cache River is floatable almost any time, but be cautious when the water is high. Water levels do fall fairly quickly after heavy rains though. Expect hazards blocking your path and the occasional need to portage.

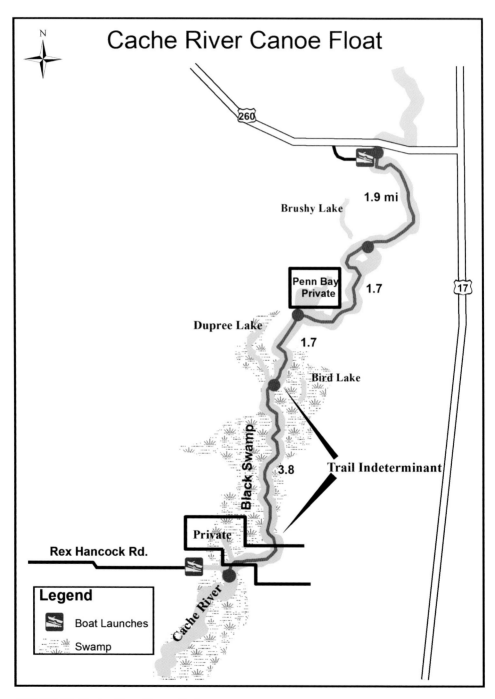

FIGURE 57: Cache River Canoe Trail.

The Cache River tends to have long stretches of open water interspersed with areas of swamp. In the swamp forest areas, the river is often highly braided, with multiple routes possible. Basic route-finding skills are recommended for doing any sections of the river upstream from the Black Swamp. It is not really possible to get lost since you can always follow the current downstream. However, if you take the more difficult routes through the braided sections, you could add several miles to the distances given.

The following Cache River routes are continuous: the ending of one is the start of the next. The scenery is quite similar to the float trips described in the previous section. All are relatively remote and explorers should exercise proper outdoor precautions.

ROUTE 18 TO RAILROAD TRACK ROAD. DISTANCE: 5.6 MILES

To reach Route 18, take exit 85 off of limited-access Highway 67 and turn right (east) onto Route 18. Follow for 11.3 miles until you reach the Cache River (35.649311 N, 91.056224 W). The launch is on the east bank of the river, downstream of the road. To reach Railroad Track Road, take exit 85 off of Highway 67 and turn right (east) onto Route 18. Follow for 8.3 miles and turn right onto County Road 40/Railroad Track Road. Follow this road for 3.4 miles until you come to the Cache River. The launch is located on the west bank of the river, upstream side of the road (35.604464 N, 91.112306 W).

Upstream from Route 18 the river has been ditched and is not particularly interesting. Downstream it follows its natural course and makes for a scenic float. However, the famous Cache River logjam is found 2.0 miles downstream from this launch blocking your path, and it is not possible to complete this route at this time. Plans have been approved to remove it in the near future.

RAILROAD TRACK ROAD TO ROUTE 14. DISTANCE: 5.3 MILES

To reach Route 14, take exit 80 off of Highway 67 and turn right (east) onto Route 14. Go 6.7 miles until you come to the river where the launch is on the west bank, downstream side of the road (35.563049 N, 91.141371 W).

This section is fairly short and easy, although the river is quite winding. Several areas of the river are braided allowing for a variety of pathways.

ROUTE 14 TO ROUTE 145. DISTANCE: 6.3 MILES

To reach Route 145, take exit 80 off of Highway 67 and turn right (east) onto Route 14. Go 4.7 miles and turn right (south) onto Route 145. Follow Route 145 for 7.9 miles until you cross the river. The boat launch is located on the east bank of the river, downstream side of the road (35.470362 N, 91.134035 W).

This section is winding and has several sections of narrow braided channels to navigate.

ROUTE 145 TO ROUTE 33. DISTANCE: 11.1 MILES

To reach Route 33, take exit 55 off of Highway 67 at Bald Knob and turn right (east) onto Route 64. Go 12.6 miles to the town of Augusta. Turn left (north) onto Route 33 and follow for 16.7 miles until you come to the river. The launch is located on the east bank of the river, downstream side of the road (35.371281 N, 91.175681 W).

This section is long but rather straightforward. Much of it is open water, and there are few braided sections to navigate

ROUTE 33 TO ROUTE 17. DISTANCE: 4.4 MILES

To reach Route 17, take exit 55 off of Highway 67 at Bald Knob. Go right (east) on Route 64 for 22.3 miles and turn left (north) on Route 17. Travel for 4.9 miles to where the road crosses the river. The launch is located on the east bank of the river, upstream side of the road (35.338203 N, 91.205248 W).

This short and scenic section makes for a nice short canoe trip. Several parts require some route finding.

ROUTE 17 TO HOLDER ACCESS. DISTANCE: 3.4 MILES

To reach the Holder Access, take exit 55 off of Highway 67 at Bald Knob. Go right (east) on Route 64 for 22.3 miles and turn left (north) onto Route 17. Travel 6.7 miles, passing by Route 17 access (see previous trip), and turn left (south) onto County Road 267 (or County Road 26 on some maps). Travel on this gravel road for 2.4 miles and turn left at the sign for Holder Access. Travel 0.5 miles until you reach the launch (35.315353 N, 91.225748 W).

This section goes through extensive swamps and requires much route finding.

HOLDER ACCESS TO ROUTE 260. DISTANCE: 11.8 MILES

To reach Route 260, see the "Cache River Canoe Float" in the previous section of the book.

This section is long but mostly open water with only a little route finding necessary. Along the way, you will cross under Route 64, but unfortunately there is no boat launch available at that point to break up this long stretch.

ROUTE 260 TO THE BLACK SWAMP

See previous section describing the "Cache River Canoe Float."

BLACK SWAMP CANOE TRAIL

See following section describing the "Black Swamp Canoe Trail."

CANOE ROUTES DOWNSTREAM OF THE BLACK SWAMP

Once downstream of the Black Swamp, there are few boat launches (none public) until you near Interstate 40. Because of the extremely long distances and lack of pubic launches and places to camp, nonmotorized travel on the Cache River downstream of the Black Swamp is not recommended.

REX HANCOCK BLACK SWAMP
WILDLIFE MANAGEMENT AREA
ARKANSAS GAME AND FISH COMMISSION

The Rex Hancock Black Swamp WMA protects several small tracts of bottomland forest and swamp forest along the middle Cache River between Augusta and Little Dixie, and is surrounded by the Cache River NWR. Only the tract due east of the small town of Gregory is accessible by car. The section of the Cache River where the Black Swamp is located is minimally modified and therefore still functions as a natural system. There is a fairly high diversity of forest types with a good selection of tree species and an especially high diversity of oaks. Wildlife abundance is high, and the Black Swamp is one of the best places for winter waterfowl. There are several old-growth stands of tupelo/cypress forest within the WMA, and some trees are probably over one thousand years old.

Since there is no camping allowed within the Cache River NWR, the Black Swamp WMA provides the only camping sites in the area. The best campsites are near the end of the road at the Railroad Dump Access/Rex Hancock Road at Gregory. These sites tend to provide a cacophony of sounds emanating from the swamp at night. There are no facilities so bring all supplies.

Dr. Archibald Rex Hancock, for whom the wildlife management is named, founded the Citizens Committee to Save the Cache and was instrumental in the preservation of the Cache River by stopping the channelization scheme that would have destroyed it. His ashes were scattered in the swamp forest adjacent to the boat ramp at the access road at Gregory and a small memorial marks the location.

BLACK SWAMP HIKING TRAIL (UNOFFICIAL)

DISTANCE: 1.0 mile one-way
TIME: 30 minutes
DIFFICULTY: easy

DIRECTIONS: There are few places to hike along the northern reaches of the Cache River, and this is not really a hiking trail per se. The trail follows the access road from the Gregory entrance through the wildlife management area and passes through some beautiful forest. Wildlife viewing is consistently good. To access the trail, follow Route 33 south from Augusta for 9.0 miles. Turn left (east) onto County Road 752 (first street in the town of Gregory), where a sign indicates the Rex Hancock/Black Swamp WMA. Follow the road for 1.5 miles and turn right onto County Road 745 (Railroad Dump Access/Rex Hancock Road), where another sign marks the refuge entrance. Follow this road until it enters the forest where a small parking area is located on the left (35.151941 N, 91.288420 W).

FIGURE 58: Cypress swamp near Maple Slough along Black Swamp Hiking Trail.

This is not really a traditional trail, but instead it follows the access road into the Black Swamp (fig. 59). It passes through several different types of forest, and plant diversity is quite high. Bird observation is especially good, and since the road offers good views into the canopy of the forest, it is an excellent place to view neotropical migrants, especially in late April into May when many are arriving from their southern wintering grounds. Waterfowl are fairly common, and it seems as if there is always at least one barred owl in attendance along the road. The trail provides an excellent overview of the basic forest types found in the Big Woods and is an easy walk for those who do not wish to get their feet wet.

Beginning at the entrance sign of the wildlife management area to 0.2 miles, the left (north) side of the trail is typical bottomland forest while the right (south) side is private land. As you look to the north, some typical trees visible include sycamore, sweet gum, black gum, willow oak, swamp chestnut oak, overcup oak, Shumard oak, and water oak. The forest has a good diversity of vines as well, including poison ivy, grapevine, and some large greenbriers. At the 0.2 mile mark, the bottomland forest transitions into a cypress/tupelo swamp. Most of the trees are small, indicating that this forest was harvested in the recent past, unlike some areas deeper in the Black Swamp that have some old-growth stands. Check the standing water carefully, and you are likely to see tadpoles from the many species of frogs that utilize the swamp as a breeding site.

By 0.3 miles there is public land on both sides of the road, dominated by cypress/tupelo swamp and soon you come to Maple Slough, which passes under the road. Wading birds can sometimes be seen in the area feeding on the small fish that inhabit the creek. Note the dark brown tea-colored water of the swamp forest. The coloration is produced by the decay of leaves from the trees, a process that releases tannic acid. This natural acidity inhibits bacterial growth so that the water is actually rather pure, although it does not look very clean.

The swamp forest continues to the 0.5 mile mark where a slight rise in the land causes a transition into bottomland forest similar to what was seen at the first section of the trail. Most of the forest here is made up of very young trees. At the 0.4 mile mark a small section of upland forest emerges. A stand of loblolly pines (*Pinus taeda*), not native to this part of the state and obviously planted, can be seen here. On the south side of the road there is a small camping area and behind it an open field.

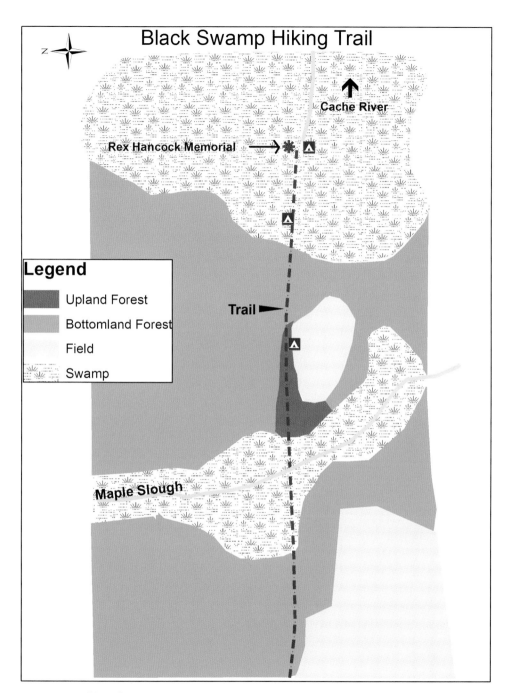

FIGURE 59: Black Swamp Hiking Trail.

Good observations of the grassland birds and disturbance-dependent species are likely here (fig. 60). The small hardwood trees around the campground are Chinquapin oaks (*Quercus muehlenbergii*), also a species not commonly seen in this area and probably planted sometime in the past.

By the 0.7 mile mark, the forest transitions back into bottomland forest with significant numbers of willow oak present, and by 0.8 miles more swamp forest is visible. The camping area on the north side of the road is one of the prettiest in the area and overlooks a nice stand of cypress trees standing in shallow water. The swamp forest dominates to the end of the trail at 1.0 miles, where the boat launch and larger camping area is located. If you are visiting in the springtime, note the native copper iris (*Iris fulva*), with its pretty dark red flowers growing by the roadside ditch and other areas in the swamp. Opposite of the campground, is the memorial to Dr. Rex Hancock.

FIGURE 60: Dickcissil (*Spiza americana*). Courtesy of Richard Hines and the US Fish and Wildlife Service.

DISTANCE: 3.4 miles
TIME: 2 hours
DIFFICULTY: moderate

DIRECTIONS: This very pretty canoe trail makes a good short trip through a high-quality tupelo/cypress swamp. To reach the upstream access, follow directions to the Railroad Dump Access/Rex Hancock Road of the Black Swamp WMA described in the previous section. To reach the downstream takeout, follow Route 33 south from Gregory for 1.5 miles. Turn left (east) onto County Road 15, where the large sign indicates the Black Swamp access. Follow the road for 1.8 miles until it ends at the boat ramp (35.130145 N, 91.311330 W). A small camping area is available here, although the ones at Rex Hancock Road are more pleasant. The downstream takeout can only be reached under fairly high water conditions, unless you are willing to drag your boat through a lot of mud.

This canoe trail is perhaps the most attractive short trip in the Big Woods and explores some impressive old-growth swamp forest (fig. 62). During fairly high water the trail is an easy float, but during low water the downstream takeout may require you to drag your canoe through the swamp a significant distance or a return paddle upstream. Wildlife is abundant, and all lands along this canoe trail are public.

From the boat ramp at the Railroad Dump Access/ Rex Hancock Road, follow a man-made canal for 0.2 miles until you reach the Cache River. Turn right and follow the river downstream. The river is bordered by extensive areas of tupelo/cypress swamp, with some impressive stands of old-growth forest featuring ancient trees, as well as some scattered bottomland forest where the land is slightly higher. The relative inaccessibility of this forest presumably led to its survival over the years. Around the first bend in the river, a small cove appears on the right, and within that cove is an unusual tupelo whose base resembles a rather scary face, and hence is referred to as the "face tree." Although clearly a natural growth pattern, it leads to a particularly spooky look as it stares at you as you paddle by (fig. 61).

Continue downstream a little over 1.0 mile, where the river is rather open. At mile 1.4, however, it narrows significantly and becomes

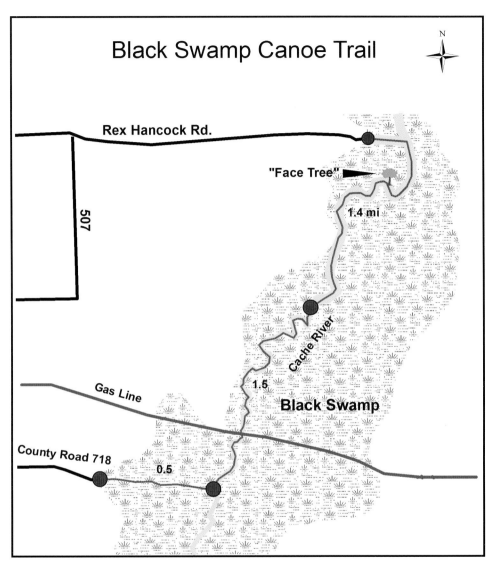

Black Swamp Canoe Trail

N

Rex Hancock Rd.

507

"Face Tree"

1.4 mi

Cache River

Gas Line

1.5

Black Swamp

County Road 718

0.5

FIGURE 62: Black Swamp Canoe Trail.

left, FIGURE 61: "Face tree," an unusually shaped water tupelo in the Black Swamp WMA.

a braided channel. The current will pick up, and although the exact route may not be clear, by following the current downstream you will be heading in the right direction. Some sandbars and stumps are present, so caution is recommended, although this stretch is not particularly hazardous. As the river narrows further, some very good stands of old-growth tupelo/cypress forest appear, mostly on the west bank (right), with several cypress trees in the one-thousand-year-old range. During high water, it is possible to canoe directly into the swamp and get close to the massive trees.

At mile 2.9, the downstream exit will appear on the right (west). It is marked with yellow tags, which will lead you to the boat launch. However, this exit is easy to navigate only during high water. At low water, the canal dries out almost completely and you will have to get out and drag the canoe. In this case, prepare for a muddy adventure, although much of the swamp has a surprisingly firm base (with scattered areas that definitely do not!). During my expeditions in 2012, several small beaver dams were present on the canal, which required portage to proceed, but those can change rapidly depending on the beaver activity. After 0.5 miles in the creek, a small pond appears and just beyond that the boat ramp (total 3.4 miles). The swamp forest just to the north of the ramp is some the best and, during high water, is excellent for exploring in your canoe. If you intend on getting some distance from the boat ramp or the access trail, do carry a compass or GPS.

SHEFFIELD NELSON DAGMAR
WILDLIFE MANAGEMENT AREA
ARKANSAS GAME AND FISH COMMISSION

The Sheffield Nelson Dagmar WMA (often referred to just as "Dagmar") is a special area of the Big Woods. Although located not far from "civilization" and bisected by Interstate 40, it boasts some of the most spectacular and probably the largest areas of old-growth forest in the entire Big Woods. Some of the oldest trees in the eastern United States, ancient bald cypress, exist here, and they are easily accessible with a canoe, kayak, or flat-bottomed johnboat. Two of the best floats in the Big Woods are also found here.

Sheffield Nelson, for whom this area is named, is from nearby Brinkley and was once head of the Arkansas Game and Fish Commission. He was instrumental in obtaining this land for public use. This conservation area is easily accessible from a network of gravel roads maintained by the Arkansas Game and Fish Commission. The commission has also been promoting nature exploration of Dagmar and has marked many canoe and hiking routes, including several that are explained in this volume. The entrance is off of Route 70 west of Brinkley (fig. 63). During times of high water, practically the entire area is under water and accessible only by boat.

4 ➤ BAYOU DEVIEW SWAMP CANOE TRAIL

DISTANCE: 7.1 miles
TIME: 6 hours minimum
DIFFICULTY: moderate to difficult, basic
route-finding skills necessary

DIRECTIONS: *This all-day canoe trip passes through the best tupelo/ cypress swamp in Arkansas, and one of the best in the United States. Basic navigation skills are required and canoe experience is recommended before tackling this route. If attempted in winter, be sure to carry a change of clothes in a dry bag in case of accidental immersion. A shuttle is necessary. To reach the trailhead, take the Route 49/17 exit off of Interstate 40 at Brinkley. Turn left and follow the road north. After about 1.5 miles, turn left onto Route 17 north. Travel about 3.0 miles to the bridge crossing Bayou DeView (34.935689 N, 91.240918 W). There is a parking area on the west bank of the bayou, on the downstream side of the bridge. For the shuttle vehicle, from Brinkley, take Route 49/17 south (right) at the interstate exit. Route 70 west will join this road just past the downtown Brinkley. Travel about 1.0 mile and go right (east), staying on Route 70. Follow Route 70 west for about 7.0 miles. Turn right at the second sign for Dagmar (not the Apple Lake turn). Follow the gravel road for about 2.0 miles and turn right at the clearly marked road for Bayou DeView. The road ends in about 1.0 mile, which is where your canoe trip will terminate (34.859033 N, 91.290452 W).*

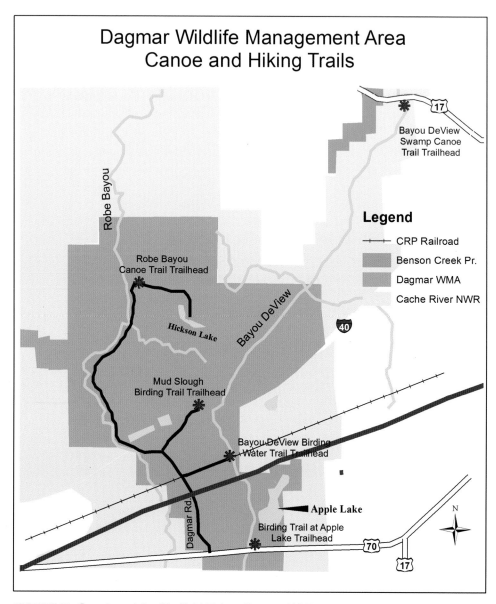

FIGURE 63: Overview of the Sheffield Nelson Dagmar WMA, showing access points and trailheads.

The Bayou DeView Swamp is my favorite canoe trail in the Big Woods and will take you through a spectacular tupelo/cypress habitat (fig. 64). By all appearances, most areas of this swamp have never been harvested and therefore represent an old-growth forest. About 90 percent of the trees are water tupelo. The remainder are mostly bald cypress, including many giants that according to tree ring analysis are up to 1,200 years old (Spond 2007). Some areas have been selectively harvested in the past, but most of the swamp was untouched by the axe. Bayou DeView represents one of the best examples of a pristine tupelo/cypress swamp in the entire United States. A trip through this site is an almost other-worldly experience and has a definite prehistoric feel to it as you travel through giant trees growing in the murky water. Wildlife is fairly abundant, although bird life is not as prolific as you might expect. The bottomland forests actually have a lot more wildlife, but for a botanical experience there is none better than Bayou DeView.

A few precautions are in order for this trip. You will at least need a compass and many will prefer to carry a GPS. I have included GPS coordinates for important landmarks along the float. This trip should be attempted when water levels are moderate, which means there should be at least one foot of water in the forest at your launching, not just in the main channel. Under such conditions, a small amount of current will be present, which helps in navigation, and there will be fewer obstacles. Low water makes this trip a difficult one, and in all likelihood you will not get very far if only the main channel contains water. The US Geological Survey has recently installed a water gauge on Bayou DeView. If it is at 14 feet or higher, it is possible to canoe the length of this water trail. During the dry season, it is possible to walk around through the swamp since much of the ground is surprisingly firm. Ownership of this land is complex, with various parts owned by the Nature Conservancy (private conservation), Cache River NWR (federal), and Dagmar WMA (state of Arkansas).

Begin your trip at the Route 17 bridge, where there is a primitive launch on the west side of the bayou (fig. 65). Paddle out into the main channel, which in this section is a small open water lake. The west side (right) of this lake is the Benson Creek Preserve, owned by the Nature Conservancy. Former bottomland forest areas of this preserve, just to the west, are being reforested with native trees while the lowland areas

are made up of mature swamp forest, most never harvested. After 0.15 miles the lake narrows to a small but easily visible channel. It is at this point that the grandeur of this forest first becomes evident. Large bald cypress are interspersed amongst dense stands of water tupelo. Look carefully and you will see that many are tall, straight trees that would have been valuable to loggers. Most large surviving cypress found today are hollow, crooked, and of little commercial value. For some reason this forest was spared though, a small remnant of the millions of acres that once covered the southeast United States.

Follow the narrow channel to the 2.0 mile mark. The channel is quite easy to follow as it curves through the trees. Usually there is enough current to push you along. This section is probably the prettiest along the entire canoe trail. After you have passed through the forest, a small lake will appear as the channel curves a little to the west (34.916372 N, 91.254499 W). On the west side of this lake, there is a small creek, Benson Slash Creek, in which you can paddle upstream for some distance, and which the Nature Conservancy has been instrumental in protecting. The habitat is similar to that found along Bayou DeView. The Nature Conservancy has reforested land around the creek and also undertaken a restoration project where a ditched section of Benson Slash Creek was engineered back to its original natural course. This restoration and reforestation should improve water quality throughout the Bayou DeView region.

Just opposite of where Benson Slash Creek enters the lake is an unusual pair of tupelo trees fused about twenty feet off the surface of the water. This fusion results in the trees having an "H" shape, one of the more unusual tree shapes you are likely to see anywhere. If you are not using a shuttle, it is probably best to turn around here and head back to the Route 17 crossing, but realize you will be paddling against the current.

The lake decreases in width down to a fairly narrow stretch at the south end (mile 2.4), where there are two distinct channels. You can take either (the right one is more direct), and at mile 2.6 you will enter a power line right-of-way. Here the main channel of the creek turns right along the power line and reenters the forest near the far west

left, FIGURE 64: Bayou DeView Swamp during the dry season. Cache River NWR.

side of the swamp. It is not entirely clear where the channel is, but it is best to follow the area with the strongest current. As you reenter the forest, it quickly becomes a maze of tupelo trees. In general, paddle in a south-southwest direction. At mile 3.5, you will come to the next lake (34.899595 N, 91.262870 W). At the south end of this lake at mile 3.7 is the border for the Dagmar WMA, which you will remain in for the rest of the trip. Most of the previous habitat has been in the Cache River NWF.

From this point on, the "trail" is basically a maze through flooded swamp forest. There is no obvious route, and the swamp becomes very wide in this area, up to 1.5 miles. (Note, since I last scouted this trail, the Arkansas Game and Fish Commission has placed trail markers on the trees. However, if you get off the marked trail, the following directions will help you find the way.) In general, follow a southwest direction, and if you travel too far east or west, you will reach dry ground. Although there is no obvious trail, there is still a faint current that generally goes in the direction you need to travel, so if in doubt follow the current. Floating dead timber probably will require you to paddle away from the trail anyway. The forest in this section is very nice with lots of old-growth characteristics. Undoubtedly, the inaccessibility of this swamp made it difficult for loggers to reach the large cypress trees. This section is quite long, about 2.3 miles if you can maintain a relatively straight course, but numerous logjams and subsequent detours will probably extend your trip.

As you travel southwest, the swamp becomes progressively narrower and the noise from Interstate 40 becomes louder, indicating that you are about to emerge from the swamp. The current gets stronger, and a few open-water areas appear at mile 6.0 (34.878185 N, 91.286532 W). As you approach the interstate, two larger lakes appear, and you can follow either of these, although the one on the left is easier. You will now come to the interstate (mile 6.3, 34.869526 N, 91.291472 W). Turn to the right (west) and follow the bayou under the bridge (mile 6.4), being careful with the swift current caused by the interstate construction that narrowed the channel.

Once under the bridge, Bayou DeView turns slightly southeast, but if in doubt, stay in the current. Follow the bayou to mile 7.1 until you see the old railroad bridge, now in ruins (34.859639 N, 91.288257 W). Just

Bayou DeView Swamp Canoe Trail

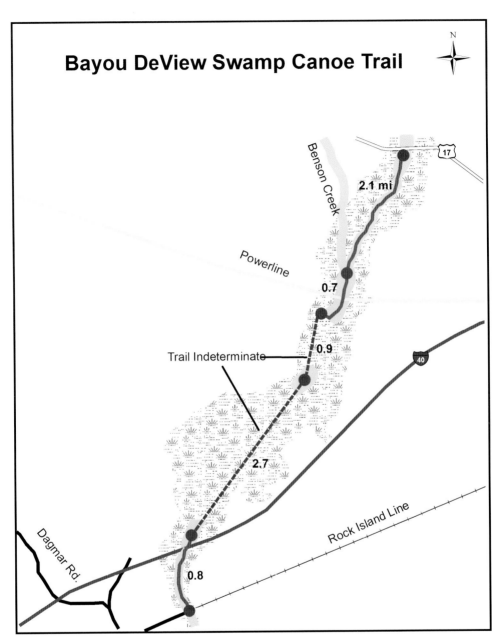

FIGURE 65: Bayou DeView Swamp Canoe Trail.

before the railroad bridge, there is a really large cypress tree, perhaps the largest one along this entire trip. It is certainly over one thousand years old. The railway bridge you see was once part of the Chicago, Rock Island and Pacific Railroad, more commonly known as the Rock Island Line. This important railway company was made famous by a folk song originally sung by Arkansas prisoners (recorded by famed musicologist Alan Lomax) and recorded by numerous musicians, including Arkansas native Johnny Cash (Unterberger, 1997). Once you reach the railway bridge, turn right, staying on the upstream side of the bridge, and follow the bridge to your shuttle at mile 7.2. You have now completed one of the most beautiful canoe trails in the entire southeast United States.

Journey into the Past

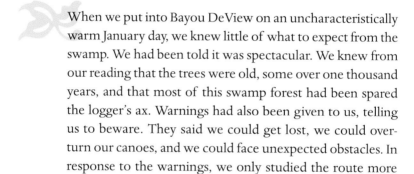

When we put into Bayou DeView on an uncharacteristically warm January day, we knew little of what to expect from the swamp. We had been told it was spectacular. We knew from our reading that the trees were old, some over one thousand years, and that most of this swamp forest had been spared the logger's ax. Warnings had also been given to us, telling us to beware. They said we could get lost, we could over-turn our canoes, and we could face unexpected obstacles. In response to the warnings, we only studied the route more carefully, scouring the satellite views and published maps.

So here we stood, January of 2012 with our canoes sit-ting in the water, paddles in hand. Just three students and one professor wondering how long it would take us to navi-gate the seven-plus miles of our planned route. The chill of the morning air was already giving way to a warming sun, and a slight southerly breeze rustled the treetops. So, with a definite sense of trepidation, we pushed off from the bank into the swamp.

We had only gone a few hundred feet when we spot-ted something in the water. Our first thought was a beaver, but when its head popped up again we saw a more interest-ing creature, a river otter. It submerged and surfaced several times, spying us carefully, seemingly unsure of what to make our two-boat flotilla. We passed, and it went back to its business of finding food while we navigated into the narrowing channel and into a tunnel of trees.

It was only a short distance before we entered the primeval forest, still within earshot of the highway and the reminder of civilization. The contrast with where we were and where we had come from was striking. We were surrounded by thousands of tupelo with their grotesquely swollen bases and their twisted trunks. Interspersed, not common at all compared to the tupelo, but making up for their relative scarcity with their immense size, were the giant bald cypress. They were the biggest we had ever seen on our scouting journeys into the Big Woods. Our excitement was hard to contain, and we paddled over to one after another just to get the sense of their sheer size. It dawned on us how we had gotten used to the "little" cypress that make up most of the Big Woods. These trees were something else entirely. This forest was something different and somehow more what a swamp forest is "supposed" to be.

We paddled on. The giant trees stretched onward mile after mile. The day continued to warm. We could have easily mistaken the day for an early April one, so warm was it for January, and we realized how lucky we were to experience this weather. In the days to come, there would no doubt be a return to wintertime. Even a few frogs, spring peepers and chorus frogs called from the swamp, also fooled by the unseasonable warmth. We wondered if even the plants might be stirring from their winter's dormancy.

Considering all the warnings we had received, the day went surprisingly smoothly. We had a few obstacles to navigate and a bit of route finding at times, but the obvious current always told us which direction to go. By late afternoon, we were at the end of our journey and back in our vehicles. We all had a great sense of accomplishment, and a sense of privilege at having seen the magnificent forest.

Later that night as we compiled our notes for the day,

the discussion turned to what the Bayou DeView swamp means to the Big Woods and the people of Arkansas. We came to the conclusion that it represents an example of what could be. All across the Big Woods, almost all the forest had been cut over at least once, if not several times. Almost all the ancient trees had long ago been removed for their valuable lumber. Most people probably had no idea what the Big Woods is really supposed to look like, since all they ever saw was the younger regenerating forest that covers most of the region. We had seen a window into the past, to a time before people came to dominate the landscape, to a time when wilderness was the norm and civilization was the "other." How sad we thought that an old-growth forest is the rarity, something that has to be fiercely protected, not so much because of is beauty, but because of its extreme rarity. Maybe though, if more people saw this place, they could understand what conservation could look like. The land, or some lands at least, would return to this state if given enough time. Maybe if we were lucky, more of the Big Woods could be restored, or should we say, allowed to return to its former glory. If not though, the big trees of Bayou DeView might stand for thousands of years more as a reminder of what once was.

DISTANCE: 1.7 miles
TIME: 2 hours
DIFFICULTY: easy

DIRECTIONS: This state-sponsored water trail goes downstream from the end of the previous canoe trail and passes through similar tupelo/cypress habitat. The trail is well marked along its entire length and there is relatively narrow area of swamp compared to the previous trail, so it is almost impossible to get lost. To reach the trailhead, follow directions for the shuttle at the end of the Bayou DeView Swamp Trail (previous section). For the shuttle for this trail, turn off Route 70 at the Apple Lake area, which is located about a quarter mile east of the main entrance to Dagmar. A parking area is located immediately after the turnoff, which is also the parking area for the Birding Trail at Apple Lake (34.840583 N, 91.282684 W).

Arkansas has recently begun to promote its flatwater canoe opportunities, and this is one of the finest of the state's official trails. For those who do not wish to do the challenging Bayou DeView trip, this one makes a pleasant and easier alternative (fig. 66). Begin where the Bayou DeView canoe trail ended at the Rock Island Line. From the parking area, paddle due east along the left side of the bridge until you reach the main channel, and turn right (south) to go under the remains of the bridge. Almost immediately you enter a loose maze of cypress and tupelo trees, although signs placed by the Arkansas Game and Fish Commission mark the trail well. Cypress trees are more common than tupelo in this section of Bayou DeView, unlike the area upstream of the interstate where tupelo are the dominant species. Most of the cypress trees are small, indicating that the area was logged in the past, but also evidence that natural reproduction has allowed the forest to grow back. After 0.7 miles, the maze opens into a small lake. On the left (east), is an old elevated road that is also a short hiking trail (Birding Trail at Apple Lake, see next description). To the east and across the road is Apple Lake, a small but pretty impoundment that is filled with many submerged tupelo and cypress trees. You can beach your canoe on the road and walk along the west side of the lake, which is a good spot to

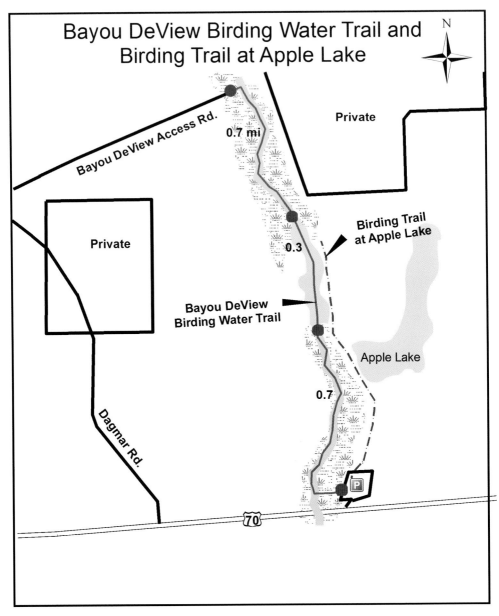

FIGURE 66: Bayou DeView Birding Water Trail.

see waterfowl. Please note that Apple Lake and the land north and east of the lake are closed as a duck rest area during waterfowl hunting season. Follow the lake south and reenter a maze of trees, this time with the trees spaced a little tighter than the previous maze. Continue to follow the trail signs, but if you get off the main trail it is simple enough to follow the current downstream. At mile 1.5, you leave the maze and enter a larger open-water area where a broken-down bridge is visible in the distance. If the water is fairly high, turn left on the upstream of the bridge side and head to the bank where your shuttle car is parked. If the water is low, you can pass under the bridge and then turn left to a parking area next to Highway 70. Alternatively, if you do not have a shuttle car parked, you can turn back to the trailhead. This will entail paddling against the current, which is usually fairly mild.

6 ➤ BIRDING TRAIL AT APPLE LAKE

DISTANCE: 1.4 miles round-trip
TIME: 1 hour
DIFFICULTY: easy

DIRECTIONS: This trail begins at the Apple Lake parking area. For directions, see description for the downstream takeout of the Bayou DeView Birding Water Trail (previous section).

This short hiking trail follows an old road between Apple Lake and Bayou DeView. It offers a good opportunity to see a variety of habitats including a small lake, swamp, and bottomland forest (fig. 66). Birds are common along the entire length of the trail, and waterfowl are particularly abundant during the winter. Lands to the east of the trail, including Apple Lake (fig. 67) are closed to entry during duck season.

If the lake is not closed to entry, it is possible to canoe it as well. It is a very scenic spot with hundreds of fairly old tupelo trees. From the parking area for the trail, paddle north along a ditch for about a quarter mile. At that point, you reach the lake, and you can paddle among the submerged tupelo trees at will.

DISTANCE: 3.5 miles round-trip
TIME: 2 hours
DIFFICULTY: moderate

DIRECTIONS: This state-supported trail travels along an old road through nice bottomland forest and swamps, and it also passes a few small ponds. Good birding opportunities are available, and numerous species are likely to be seen, both wetland and forest species. Amphibians and reptiles are common in summer. From Brinkley, take Route 49/17 south through town. Route 70 west will join this road just past the downtown area. Travel about 1.0 mile and merge right, staying on Route 70. Continue west for about 7.0 miles. Turn right at the second sign for Dagmar (not the Apple Lake Turn). You will come to the Dagmar headquarters area, where there is a Y in the road. Go left toward Robe Bayou. Almost immediately, there is another Y. Go right. Follow this road under the interstate, and you will arrive at a small parking area where the trail is clearly marked (34.868411 N, 91.300500 W).

At the trailhead (fig. 68), there is a small pond that will often contain a few waterfowl. Once on the trail (about a quarter mile from trailhead), there is a pond on the right that is also a good spot for waterfowl. A small low-water bridge crosses the trail at this point where water drains from the left side of the trail into the pond, making for a cold crossing in winter if the water is high. Tall waterproof boots will be a great help in winter, but if rainfall has been low, it will be dry. Once past this point, the trail follows through overcup/Nuttall's oak bottomland forest typical of the area. Interspersed along the way are areas of swamp dominated by cypress and tupelo. None of this forest has the grandeur of some other areas of Dagmar as logging was probably extensive in the past.

The trail eventually enters a larger swamp forest area and crosses Mud Slough, a small creek that flows west into Robe Bayou. During wet times, the area around the trail will be flooded, but the trail itself

FIGURE 67: View from the Bayou DeView Birding Trail with water tupelo submerged in Apple Lake. Dagmar WMA.

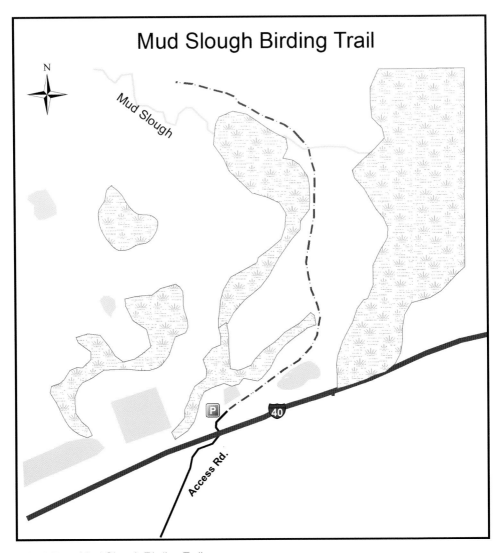

Mud Slough Birding Trail

N

Mud Slough

P 40

Access Rd.

FIGURE 68: Mud Slough Birding Trail.

is elevated enough to stay dry in almost all weather. The trail turns left and passes through good quality bottomland forest until it abruptly ends. During times of low water, you can wander about the forest here and see some typical bottomland forest dominated by overcup oaks. Birding tends to be better near the end of the trail where there is a nice variety of habitats and the sound of the interstate is more distant. Return the way you came to get back to the parking area.

Upstream from the Bayou DeView Swamp Canoe Trail are many more miles that can be traversed, much of the area also very beautiful habitat. Like other trails in Bayou DeView, some basic canoeing experience is recommended, and you must pay close attention to water levels. All the areas described are best traveled when there is moderate flow in Bayou DeView. Distances are all approximate, since beaver dams, dead floating timber, and other obstacles will require frequent navigational adjustments. Extreme caution should always be taken on Bayou DeView, since help would be far away if there was an emergency, and outside of duck season there are very few people on these waters. All the routes upstream from Route 17 are managed by the Cache River NWR, but always keep in mind there is much private land inholdings throughout.

ROUTE 38 TO ROUTE 17. DISTANCE: 7.8 MILES

Directions to Route 17 are described in the previous section on the Bayou DeView Swamp Canoe Trail. To reach the Route 38 crossing, follow Route 49 north from Brinkley for 7.5 miles. Turn left (west) on Route 38, and follow it for 3.4 miles. A primitive launch is available on the west bank of the bayou, upstream side of the road with adequate parking for several cars (35.005287 N, 91.207994 W). A new bridge is being built over Bayou DeView, so details of the boat launch could change in the future.

This long, moderately challenging route is similar the Bayou DeView Swamp Trail and involves some route-finding skills. It is extremely scenic.

ROUTE 306 TO ROUTE 38. DISTANCE: 5.0 MILES

To reach the Route 306 crossing, go west from the Route 38 crossing for 1.1 miles. Turn right (north) onto Route 17 for 4.1 miles. Turn right (east) onto Route 306 and travel 2.1 miles. The primitive launch is on the west bank of the bayou, downstream side of the road, but there is room for only one or two cars to park (35.061545 N, 91.202805 W).

This section is a bit easier to follow than the previous one described, but still involves some route finding through a couple of areas.

ROUTE 145 TO ROUTE 306. DISTANCE: 9.6 MILES

To reach the Route 145 crossing, go west from the Route 306 crossing for 2.1 miles. Turn right (north) onto Route 17 and go 5.6 miles to Route 260. Turn right (east) and go 6.8 miles until the junction with Route 145. At junction, go straight (you are now on Route 145) for 1.2 miles. A primitive boat launch is located on the east bank of the bayou, downstream side of the road, but there is limited parking (35.155744 N, 91.136551 W).

This difficult and long section should only be attempted by experienced paddlers. It is also not recommended in cold weather, since help would be far away in case of an accident.

ROUTE 64 TO ROUTE 145. DISTANCE: 9.0 MILES

To get to the Route 64 crossing, go east from the Route 145 crossing for 3.8 miles. Turn left (north) onto Route 269, and go 8.2 miles. At Route 64, turn left and travel 1.1 miles. The primitive boat launch is on the west bank of the bayou, upstream side of the road with room for several cars (35.252043 N, 91.111303 W).

This section is long, but not quite as difficult as the one described previously. Nonetheless, basic route-finding methods will be necessary through many areas. Upstream from this point, Bayou DeView is ditched and not an attractive canoeing area.

NEW ARKANSAS GAME AND FISH TRAILS

The Arkansas Game and Fish Commission has recently added additional official canoe trails within Dagmar WMA that I have not had the opportunity to explore. These are well marked along their entire length. These include a route from Hickson Lake (fig. 63) to Bayou DeView, and a moderately long route south of Highway 70, also along Bayou DeView. The route from Hickson Lake can be explored only in relatively high water, while the Bayou DeView route south of Highway 70 typically has good water flow throughout more of the year, but can still be impassable during moderately dry times. Information on these trails can be obtained at the Arkansas Game and Fish Commission website under the Watchable Wildlife Program (See appendix 2). Interpretive signs at the trailheads also provide descriptions of the routes.

DISTANCE: 3.5 miles one-way
TIME: 3 hours
DIFFICULTY: moderate (some portages likely)

DIRECTIONS: This canoe route passes through some small but excellent stands of old-growth cypress trees. This is a state-sponsored water trail. In Brinkley take Route 49/17 south through town. Route 70 west will join this road just past the downtown area. Travel about 1.0 mile and merge right, staying on Route 70. Stay on Route 70 west for about 7.0 miles. Turn right at the second sign for Dagmar (not the Apple Lake Turn). You will come to the Dagmar headquarters. Go left and follow the road under the interstate. Robe Bayou now appears on the left. There are numerous launch spots along the left side of the road as it parallels the bayou. If you wish to paddle the entire water trail, follow the road for 3.0 miles to where the road makes a sharp right turn away from the bayou. The small parking area here is the last access point to the water trail (34.894635 N, 91.314170 W). For a shuttle, you can leave another car at any of the other launch locations.

Robe Bayou is a relatively long narrow body of water that branches from the Cache River near Cotton Plant. It flows downstream for about 20.0 miles and then joins Bayou DeView just before it flows back into the Cache River. The section described here is floatable under most conditions and passes through some beautiful forest, including some areas of old-growth cypress (fig. 69). The lower section close to Interstate 40 is floatable even under drought conditions. From the trailhead (fig. 70), launch into a small lake from which you can travel upstream or downstream. Upstream, the bayou becomes narrow and choked with vegetation and is often blocked by beaver dams. Although possibly passable, it would be a difficult journey. Instead, we will go downstream. The small lake quickly narrows and makes a sharp right turn at 0.3 miles. At this turn is a great cluster of huge cypress trees, some of the largest on this trail, growing in the middle of the bayou. Paddle your canoe between the trees, sometimes a difficult endeavor if debris is jammed among the cypress knees. For the next 1.2 miles, you will canoe through some of the prettiest swamp in all of Arkansas. Many large bald cypress are present, with a smattering of water tupelo growing among them. Along this

stretch of the bayou, you will likely encounter several portages where the water is blocked by vegetation and sometimes by beaver activity. The extra work is well worth it to experience the beauty of this spot.

The surrounding land is covered with bottomland forest at a somewhat higher elevation (just a few feet higher) than the other areas of Dagmar. Some good stands of willow oak are found here along with interspersed Nuttall's oak, overcup oak, sweet gum, and sugarberry. The banks of Robe Bayou often have good stands of native bamboo, which is the preferred habitat of the relatively rare Swainson's warbler. It should be noted that bottomland forest dominated by willow oaks has become a rare habitat in the Big Woods.

At mile 1.0, a low-water bridge crosses the creek. Beach your canoe just upstream at the parking area and portage around. The bayou should be easier to float from this point on, and no more portages are needed. For the next 0.5 miles, the bayou remains narrow but then opens up into a long narrow lake. From here the trees get noticeably smaller. Most likely the open water of this section allowed for easy access for loggers in the past, so all the cypress trees here are secondary growth. Waterfowl are more common in this part of the bayou compared to previous sections. During windy conditions, canoeing in this area can be difficult. The trail remains in this open lake until it reaches the interstate at mile 3.5. Although not as scenic as the narrow upper part of the bayou, it makes for an easy low-key float with good chances to see wildlife. You should also walk around the bottomland forest anywhere along the water trail. Some of the forested areas are impressive, and the relatively high ground is almost always easy to traverse.

MIKE FREEZE WATTENSAW WILDLIFE MANAGEMENT AREA

Located on the west bank of the White River, Wattensaw protects a large area of upland forest as well as significant sections of bottomland forest and swamps (fig. 71). Unlike most other protected areas in the Big Woods, flooding is not likely in most of Wattensaw, and it is usually accessible all year. If the rest of the Big Woods is in heavy

FIGURE 69: Canoeists on Robe Bayou among the ancient cypress trees.

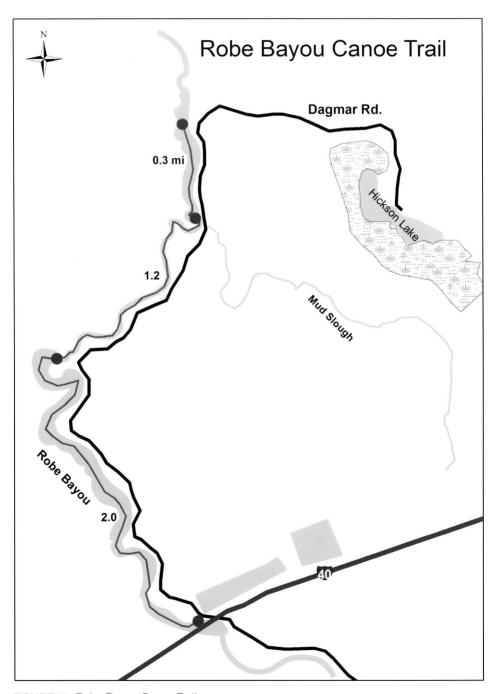

FIGURE 70: Robe Bayou Canoe Trail.

GUIDE TO VISITING THE BIG WOODS

flood, Wattensaw will provide some dry ground to explore. Most of the forests are located on the Grand Prairie Terrace, a slightly elevated land that supports an entirely different plant community compared to other regions of the Big Woods (see fig. 19). There are many primitive campsites along the roads throughout, especially along Fire Tower Road and Fawn Acres Road. However, for the best camping experience, you should spend a night at the "Riverside Camp" at the end of Robinson Road in the northeast corner of the management area (labeled on fig. 71). This beautiful site is perched on a high bluff overlooking the White

Wattensaw WMA

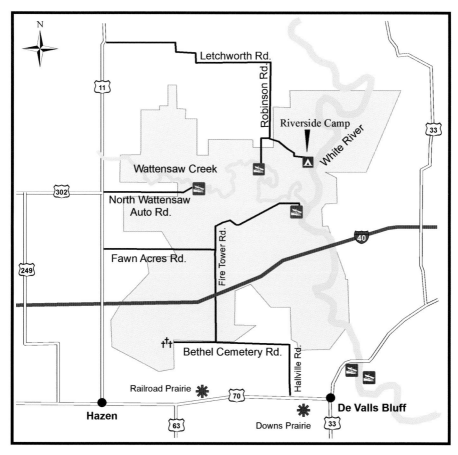

FIGURE 71: Overview of Mike Freeze Wattensaw WMA.

River, providing a great view where you can watch the water slowly roll downstream. All campsites are primitive, and you must provide all supplies, including potable water. Wattensaw is closed to nonhunters during modern gun and muzzleloader season for safety reasons. The nearest supplies can be found at Hazen or DeValls Bluff, just south of Interstate 40, or north of the management area at Des Arc.

I have described one water trail and one hiking trail. There are numerous ATV trails, primarily designed for mobility-impaired hunters, and these all make good hiking trails outside of deer season. The farm fields surrounding Wattensaw often contain large numbers of migrating birds in the winter, particularly snow geese, which can be observed from various state and county roads. Some areas of high-quality native prairie (Railroad and Downs Prairies) are preserved just south of Wattensaw and are described in a later section of this book (See Sites Outside of the Big Woods Areas)

9 ➤ WATTENSAW BAYOU WATER TRAIL

DISTANCE: 7.8 miles
TIME: 5 hours
DIFFICULTY: moderate

DIRECTIONS: This water trail, established by the Arkansas Game and Fish Commission and the Arkansas Canoe Cub, travels down this winding bayou through extensive areas of upland forest and eventually enters the White River. A shuttle is needed to canoe the entire trail. To reach the trailhead, from Interstate 40 take exit 193 and turn north onto Route 11. Travel north 2.9 miles to North Wattensaw Auto Trail (the road sign was missing in 2013, but there is a WMA sign) and turn right. Follow for 2.4 miles, make a left turn (if you go straight it dead ends), and park at the boat launch (34.864902 N, 91.522368 W). For the shuttle, from exit 193 travel 1.4 miles north on Route 11 and turn right (east) onto County Road 708 (Fawn Acres Road.) Follow for 3.0 miles and turn left (north) at the T in the road onto Fire Tower Road. Follow this road for 3.4 miles until it ends at the White River (34.854445 N, 91.471182 W).

With its well-marked route, open water, and slight current, this trail is a great experience for beginners, although it is quite long (fig. 72). It passes through mostly upland forest interspersed with smaller areas of bottomland and swamp forest. The forest lining the bayou is a mixture of bald cypress, water tupelo, and black gum. Buttonbush is extremely abundant throughout the creek and provides excellent butterfly watching when blooming in summer. The floodplain forest, mostly a narrow strip along the bayou, has overcup oak and Nuttall's oak dominating, while the extensive upland forests consist of white oak and mockernut hickory in great abundance, with numerous other tree species in lesser numbers. Because this bayou has cut through the Grand Prairie Terrace with its upland forests and prairies, it has a very different feel to it compared to the other creeks and bayous that pass through the more typical Mississippi Alluvial Plain with the extensive bottomland forests.

From the North Road access, paddle out away from the launch until in the main channel. Hurricane Creek joins Wattensaw Creek just past the launch (0.2 miles) to the south but is not usually passable by canoe. Follow the signs placed by the Arkansas Game and Fish Commission downstream. There is very little floodplain in this section, and you can beach your canoe and get out to walk around almost anywhere, which is well worth the effort. The forest understory is fairly open, and walking is easy. Good birding can be found throughout. For the first three miles, the bayou meanders through pretty forest. Then you will come to an old railroad trestle (34.871988 N, 91.496157 W). The land in the vicinity of this structure is private, so you should stay in the canoe for this stretch of the bayou. Several houses will be seen on either side of the creek. Just past the trestle at mile 3.5 is a boat launch on the north side of the river, which is an additional shuttle location. This is the Robinson Road access, which can be reached from the north side of the wildlife management area (see fig. 71, 34.872447 N, 91.489838 W). For those wanting a shorter trip, this access is an additional way to experience the area.

Downstream from Robinson Road, the bayou becomes even more winding but also wider with a more extensive floodplain forest. During times of high water, especially when the White River is high and backs up the bayou, it is possible to paddle through the forest. The bayou becomes more open in many sections. Wildlife viewing tends to get better as you travel downstream, and birding is particularly good in the bottomland forests along the last two or three miles of the bayou. Near the end of the water trail at mile 7.4, the bayou has produced some large erosion scars in the Grand Prairie, and the thick clay characteristic of this ecoregion is evident.

Just before the end of the trail at mile 7.8, Wattensaw Bayou turns sharply to the south and parallels the White River for a short distance. Be careful not to paddle into the river as currents are usually swift and dangerous. The boat launch will soon appear on the right where the trail ends at mile 7.8.

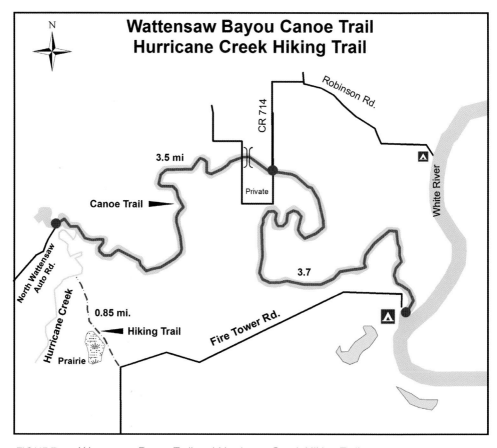

FIGURE 72: Wattensaw Bayou Trail and Hurricane Creek Hiking Trail.

DISTANCE: 1.7 miles round-trip
TIME: 45 minutes
DIFFICULTY: easy

DIRECTIONS: This trail follows an abandoned road and passes through a variety of habitats. To reach the trailhead, follow Route 11 north from Interstate 40 to Fawn Acres Road and turn right (east). Follow this road for 3.0 miles and turn left (north) on Fire Tower Road. Travel for 0.7 miles to where the road makes a sharp right turn. Park on the left by the gate (34.848435 N, 91.513268 W).

The trail (fig. 72) starts out passing through upland forest with patches of native grassland (fig. 73). Some of the forest in the first section has been actively managed (i.e. selectively logged) and is not as aesthetically pleasing as are other areas, but wildlife is abundant. The open areas support some birds (numerous sparrows) that are unlikely to be seen in a closed canopy forest. After about a quarter mile, a large

FIGURE 73: View of prairie and woodlands from the Hurricane Creek Hiking Trail.

grassland appears on the left (west) side of the trail that appears to be natural prairie. Good wildflowers can be viewed spring through fall. Just past the grassland, the land drops down a few feet, and a small area of bottomland forest appears. The dominant plant in this forest is the willow oak, which makes up a large proportion of the trees. Other common bottomland forest oaks found in other parts of the Big Woods are relatively rare here. The trail has a slight rise, and then dips again into more extensive areas of bottomland forest at mile 0.75. On the west side of the trail is a large and very pretty area of mature forest with quite a few larger trees. This type of forest extends to the banks of Hurricane Creek at 0.85 miles. The creek has a few small cypress trees. There used to be bridge over the creek, but it has been demolished. The creek always contains water, even in the driest of weather, so you have to stop here and return the way you came. During dry times, it is worthwhile to wander around the floodplain forest on the west side of the trail. The forest has almost no understory trees or shrubs and therefore no obstacles to easy travel. During the fall, the carpet of reddish-brown willow oak leaves covering the ground is very attractive.

Southern Big Woods

The southern Big Woods is the largest and wildest area. It extends from Route 79 at Clarendon, south to where the Arkansas River enters the Mississippi River (fig. 74). Access is relatively good through a network of gravel roads and extensive waterways. Since this area is far from major cities or highways, it is possible to have a near-wilderness experience in some parts of this region. One must carefully watch the water levels here as well. Rapidly rising water can flood much of the area, and it is possible to be stranded, although refuge rangers will work hard to move you out of the area before flooding makes the roads impassable. Many rare and endangered species occur in this section. In many ways, the southern section is the heart of the Big Woods and one of the last wild areas in the lower Mississippi Valley.

WHITE RIVER NATIONAL WILDLIFE REFUGE

The White River NWR protects 160,000 acres of habitat, mostly bottomland forest, along the lower White River and is the most important of all protected lands in the Big Woods (fig. 74). Typically flooded at least once per year, the White River NWR is the best example of bottomland forests in the lower Mississippi Valley. The refuge is extensive, but access is fairly good, especially in the southern section between St. Charles and the Arkansas Post Canal. The northern section from St. Charles to Clarendon has poor road access. There are hundreds of miles of waterways, lakes, bayous, and chutes in the White River NWR that allow an almost endless opportunity for exploration. Much of the forest is also fairly open, making for easy walking when the water levels are down.

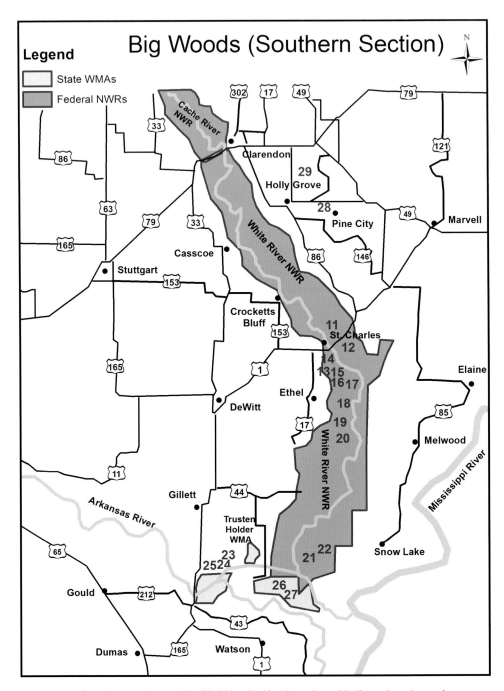

FIGURE 74: Southern section of the Big Woods. Numbers in red indicate locations of described trails.

From Clarendon at Route 79 to St. Charles at Route 1 is the North Unit of the White River NWR. Most of this land was purchased through a complex land swap with commercial interests in 1992. Access is limited, and only a few roads allow cars (most allow only ATVs or foot traffic). More extensive access is available by boat. Wildlife viewing is dependably good. It should be noted that the entire North Unit is open to duck hunters throughout the waterfowl season until 1:00 p.m. each day. During this time, which tends to correspond to the peak winter migration abundance, waterfowl observation is not as good since the animals are predictably skittish. The rest of the year, wildlife viewing is similar to that in the South Unit.

The best access is at the Brown Shanty Lake access road located off of Route 1 just east of St. Charles (fig. 75). The area contains many small lakes, some of which are connected by narrow bayous that make for rewarding exploration. Numerous ATV trails provide many routes for hiking, although they tend to be muddy much of the year.

11 ➤ LAMBERT BAYOU/SWAN LAKE FLOAT

DISTANCE: 2.4 miles one-way
TIME: 1.5 hours
DIFFICULTY: moderate

DIRECTIONS: This canoe float makes for one of the prettiest in the White River NWR and is very accessible, never getting more than a few hundred yards away from the road access. Turn left off of Route 1 east of St. Charles and follow Brown Shanty Road (fig. 14) to Swan Lake (34.410979 N, 91.126454 W).

The trail starts at Swan Lake, one of the more attractive lakes in the region (fig. 77). There are no swans likely to be seen since they are extremely rare in the Big Woods, but the lake still supports abundant wildlife. It often has many great egrets present. From the boat launch at the Swan Lake camping area, turn right and head north. Swan Lake

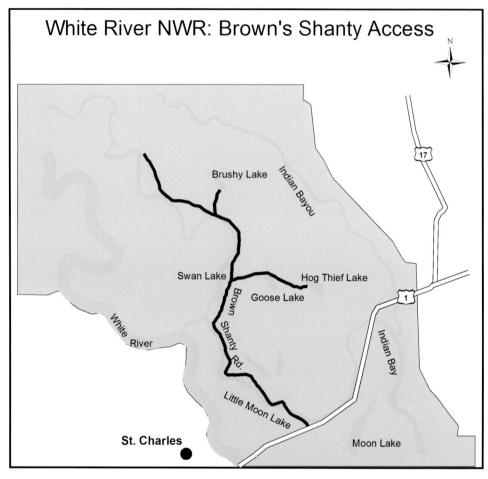

FIGURE 75: Brown Shanty access in the North Unit of the White River NWR.

is a moderately large open-water lake lined by some fairly impressive bald cypress specimens.

Once you get to the north end of the lake at mile 0.4, move to the extreme east side (right) where you will enter Lambert Bayou. The entrance to the bayou can be difficult as there are numerous button-bush specimens blocking the way, and a short portage may be necessary. After traveling about fifty yards though, the bayou opens nicely into a very beautiful waterway. Large bald cypress line the bayou, while a few old grizzled specimens grow right in the middle of the water.

FIGURE 76: Large cypress tree along Lambert Bayou. White River NWR.

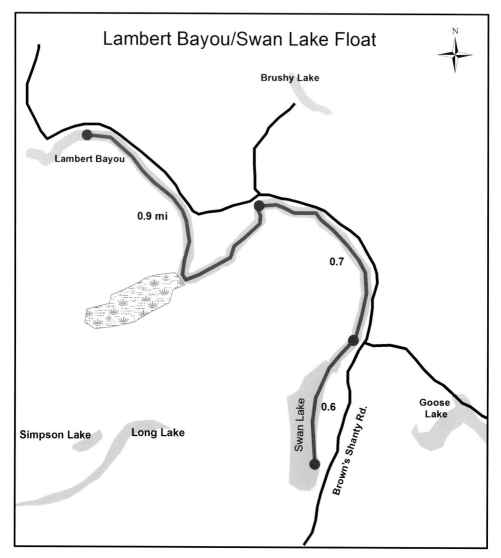

FIGURE 77: Lambert Bayou/Swan Lake Float.

At 0.6 miles, you will come to a possible landing point, which is near the road turnoff to Goose and Hog Thief Lakes. A small parking area is also available. More than likely, though, you will want to continue onward. The bayou continues to meander to the north, all the way passing among many large trees. It should be noted that during rising water, you may be paddling against the current here, but it is typically mild and not a major hindrance. At mile 1.3, there is another possible landing point that is located at the turnoff for Brushy Lake, and there is room to park a couple of vehicles.

Continuing to the north, the bayou now opens considerably, and trees get a bit smaller. At mile 1.5, the bayou turns to the west and away from the road. At 2.0 miles, you will come to an apparent T-junction (34.422682 N, 91.136163 W). To the left is a swamp area that is passable only for about one hundred yards before becoming choked with brush. Turn to the right and paddle into a substantially more open area. Here Lambert Bayou becomes more of a narrow lake. Soon the road comes back into view on the right. Follow the path to mile 2.4 where a landing is available. You can return the way you came, or if you have left a shuttle, return by road to your starting point.

Other areas to explore along the Brown's Shanty Access Road.

Brown's Shanty Road and associated side roads access several small lakes (fig. 75), all of which make for interesting canoe trips with good chances to see wildlife. Goose Lake (34.413216 N, 91.114383 W) is perhaps the most picturesque of them all and has that quintessential southern swamp appearance (fig. 78). The bald cypress that line this small

FIGURE 78: Goose Lake. White River NWR.

lake have tremendous numbers of knees protruding from the water's edge. Numerous large water tupelo are also present.

For hiking opportunities, an old driving road, now closed to all motor vehicles except ATVs, extends from the Brown's Shanty campground (34.439225 N, 91.151325 W) north for many miles. The road passes close to White River. During high water, parts of the road may be flooded, limiting your trip or requiring you to wade.

South Unit: White River NWR

Encompassing the region from Route 1 south to just north of the Arkansas River, the South Unit is accessible at several locations. The Smokehouse Hill access road at Ethel is the most important, and will allow you to explore a large section of the refuge. The southeast corner is accessed through Mellwood, which is one of the more remote areas of the Big Woods open to public use. Other access points at Route 1, Tichnor, and Indian Bay provide limited access. The South Unit of the White River NWR is by far the most impressive and wildlife rich portion of the Big Woods. You can get a real feel of wilderness in this part of the refuge, and areas of exploration are seemingly endless.

12 ➤ MOON LAKE CANOE TRAIL

DISTANCE: 4.4 miles round-trip
TIME: 3 hours
DIFFICULTY: easy (more difficult if windy)

DIRECTIONS: This large oxbow lake is located just south of the Route 1, a little east of the town of St. Charles (fig. 79). From St. Charles, follow Route 1 east for 1.5 miles. Turn right at the sign for Moon Lake. Make an immediate left and follow the gravel road 0.75 miles to the boat launch on the lake (34.382952 N, 91.094488 W).

The trip is almost all open water and not recommended on a windy day (fig. 79). The lake is accessible most of the year unless there is a major flood. During duck season, this is one of the best lakes open to the public for viewing waterfowl. Since no waterfowl hunting is allowed

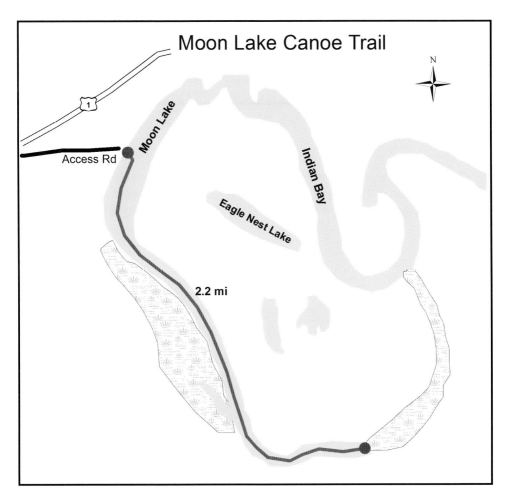

FIGURE 79: Moon Lake Canoe Trail.

here, the lake tends to support very large numbers of ducks all winter with mallards, wood ducks, and others extremely abundant. Bald eagles are also frequently in attendance.

From the boat launch, go out into the lake and turn right (south). For the first 0.5 miles, the lake is quite wide. At this point, it turns to the east and narrows considerably, although it remains open water. The east side of the lake is made up of bottomland forest, while the west side of the lake has more extensive swamp forests. Continue to mile 1.5, where a small bay appears to your left. You can paddle a short way into this bay, but it quickly becomes choked with buttonbush. During the summer, butterflies are numerous here, feeding on the rich nectar of this important swamp plant.

At mile 1.8, the lake narrows to a small bayou, but soon after it opens again into open water. Continue paddling until mile 2.2, where the lake ends. Here the right side is high ground and the left side is swamp forest. For a break from the canoe, you can easily land on the right bank and walk around to explore some high-quality bottomland forest. Ahead of you is extensive swamp forest that could theoretically be traversed by canoe all the way until you reach Indian Bayou so that you could make this a loop trail. It would be a difficult journey through the swamp, and if Indian Bayou is high, there will be significant current to paddle against in order to make the loop.

WHITE RIVER NWR VISITOR CENTER, ST. CHARLES

From the Route 1 bridge crossing the White River at St. Charles, travel 0.4 miles west toward DeWitt. Turn left (south) onto SCC Camp Road and travel one quarter mile where the visitor center will appear on the left (34.369900 N, 91.124238 W).

Situated along the White River in St. Charles is the very informative White River NWR Visitor Center (fig. 80). Interpretive displays, a bookstore, and a classroom for school groups inside the facility provide an opportunity to learn about both the natural and human history of the region. The helpful staff can answer any questions about the refuge. There are several trails near the visitor center for short hikes that will introduce the ecology and biology of the Big Woods. Several interesting specimens are available for viewing in the classroom, including a large mounted alligator gar and a massive alligator snapping turtle skeleton. The visitor center has short descriptions of the trails in the vicinity, so I have provided only a brief description of what you will find on them.

The first two trails are located right at the visitor center, while the other three are located along the Wildlife Drive, which starts just south of the parking lot. The Wildlife Drive is closed from November 1 through February 28 in order to help protect migrating waterfowl, and during this time, the trails are not open to the public. Flooding can also close the Wildlife Drive at any time, but especially in the spring.

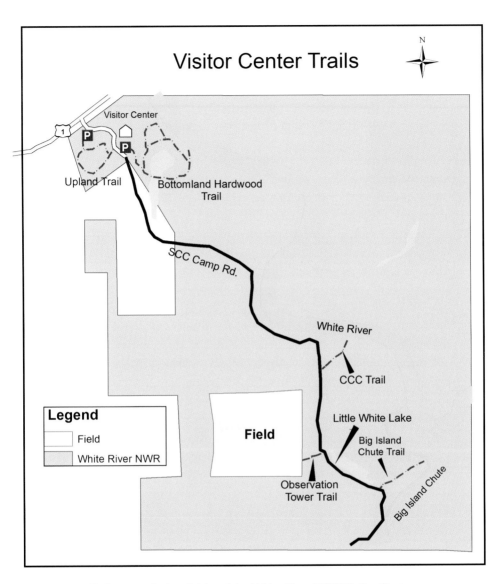

FIGURE 80: Trail system in the vicinity of the White River NWR Visitor Center.

DISTANCE: 1.5 miles round-trip, or longer if you do one of the extension loops
TIME: 1 hour
DIFFICULTY: easy (can be muddy at times)

DIRECTIONS: *Located directly behind the visitor center (fig. 80), this improved trail gives a good opportunity to see classic bottomland forest. The area was never clear cut and has some old-growth characteristics. No hunting is allowed in the vicinity, and wildlife is less wary here so that close views are easier. The trail has a long, elevated boardwalk that passes through wetland areas. You can hike out to the White River and back or follow one of two longer loops.*

The trail starts on top of the Grand Prairie Terrace but quickly drops down into bottomland forest. Most of the forest in this area was only minimally harvested in the past, and many large old trees can been seen.

The trail passes over a swamp where an elevated walkway has been built, which provides excellent wildlife viewing. If you stay quiet, you are likely to see several waterfowl species. The trail then goes back into bottomland forest where it remains until reaching the White River. Here one can get a good view of the river upstream toward St. Charles.

From this point, you can either walk back the way you came or take one of the longer loops to the north. To get to the loops, turn left and follow the orange markers that parallel the river. Signs along the way will indicate the two loops, both of which rejoin the main trail at the boardwalk where it starts over the swamp. A trail brochure is under development and should be available at the visitor center by the time of publication of this book.

DISTANCE: 1.0 mile
TIME: 45 minutes
DIFFICULTY: easy (paved)

DIRECTIONS: This paved trail starts immediately across the street from the visitor center (fig. 80) and has an additional entrance near the SCC Camp Road turnoff from Route 1.

This trail traverses upland forest situated on the Grand Prairie terrace and never floods. The forest composition is quite different from that of lowland areas. The trail also passes through several areas of grassland, once a common habitat on the Grand Prairie but now very rare. For people with limited mobility, this trail is a good choice.

DISTANCE: 1.0 mile
TIME: .5 hour
DIFFICULTY: easy

DIRECTIONS: Follow the Wildlife Drive south from the visitor center. The road will pass close to the White River where it will be visible on the left. Just past this point is the trailhead for the CCC Trail on the east side (left) of the road (34.350080 N, 91.103861 W).

This trail passes over an old levee and water-control structure built in the 1930s and ends at the White River (fig. 80). The forest is typical, but young, bottomland forest. Notable are some large sycamore and cottonwood specimens. The cottonwoods are growing directly on top of the levee and probably colonized it during construction since they prefer disturbed areas. They are very large and impressive individuals, but it is important to note that cottonwood grows very rapidly so that large trees are not particularly old.

The trail terminates at the White River, where a small bench has been installed. It is a pleasant place to sit and watch the river roll by. The fallen timbers along the edge of the river often contain many basking turtles during the warm times of the year, and several species can usually be identified if you approach them quietly.

16 ▶ OBSERVATION TOWER TRAIL

DISTANCE: .25 mile round-trip
TIME: 20 minutes
DIFFICULTY: easy

DIRECTIONS: The trail is located on the west (right) side of the road just before Little White Lake becomes visible on the east side of the road (34.342287 N, 91.104172 W).

The trail goes about two hundred yards into the woods to an observation tower that you are welcome to climb into in order to view the surrounding area (fig. 80). The forest is older bottomland forest and contains some impressive oak specimens. On the south side of the trail is a small creek lined with pretty cypress trees.

The tower overlooks a large field where wildlife is often seen. If you are there early in the morning or late in the evening, you are likely to see white-tailed deer. Open country birds are also common. Sometimes large number of snow geese can be seen in the fields, but their movements are highly variable and unpredictable.

17 ▶ BIG ISLAND CHUTE TRAIL

DISTANCE: .6 mile
TIME: 30 minutes
DIFFICULTY: easy

DIRECTIONS: Follow the Wildlife Drive past Little White Lake (which is good for waterfowl). Just past the lake on the east (left) side of the road is the trailhead (34.338028 N, 91.097892 W).

This short trail passes through bottomland forest and ends at Big Island Chute (fig. 80). There are interpretive signs along the way pointing out animals and plants common to the Big Woods. A good number of large oaks (especially Nuttall's oaks) can be seen here.

Smokehouse Hill/Ethel Access

The most extensive road system passable for regular vehicles is the Smokehouse Hill/Ethel Access (fig. 81), providing access to an extensive section of the southern Big Woods including many lakes that are excellent floats. Wildlife is very abundant, although human use is relatively high as well. There are numerous campsites available.

To reach this entrance, follow Route 17 south from St. Charles. After 6.0 miles, turn left (east) onto Ethel Road. Travel east 1.5 miles, turn right (south) onto Bisswanger Road and travel 1.5 miles Turn left (east) onto Refuge Road and travel 1.0 miles to the refuge entrance (34.264563 N, 91.120583 W).

18 ➤ BIG HORSESHOE LAKE HIKING TRAIL (UNOFFICIAL)

DISTANCE: 3.6 miles
TIME: 2 hours
DIFFICULTY: easy, but sometimes muddy in places

DIRECTIONS: This trail follows an old logging road and allows access to a large lake on one side and high-quality bottomland forest on the other. The lake is also a good canoeing or kayaking spot, but I will focus on hiking. The trail is open to ATV use, although only small numbers of people regularly use it. The Horseshoe Lake Campground is a large and pretty spot at which to camp for a few days. An improved boat launch is located at the north end of the campground. From the refuge entrance at Ethel, go straight on Big Island/Mud Lake Road and follow it 6.7 miles to the end (34.305655 N, 91.077193 W).

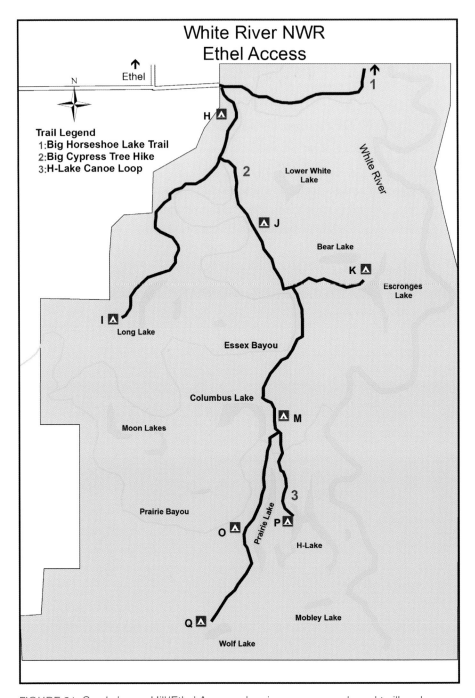

FIGURE 81: Smokehouse Hill/Ethel Access showing campgrounds and trailheads.

The trail starts at the Big Horseshoe Lake campground at the end of the road (fig. 82). A gate across the road is the start of the trail. Begin walking north. The trail follows the shoreline of Big Horseshoe Lake on the left (west), while to the right you can view good bottomland forest typical of the area. The forest here is of moderate age with a few areas of young forest that are not as majestic as the areas farther south around the Smokehouse Hill area, but still pretty enough to warrant some exploration. The trail stays in view of the lake almost the entire time, and there are good chances to see waterfowl. Many forest interior birds are common in the high-quality bottomland forest. Along this trail to the right, you will see several other ATV trails, often in various states of maintenance. These also provide a nice hike, mostly through forested areas, although I have not explored them in detail. If you decide to explore off-trail to the east, it is hard to get lost. Within a short time you will come to the White River, while the west side is blocked by Big Horseshoe Lake.

The trail follows the lake shoreline for 1.3 miles until the lake ends and a narrow bayou appears. The trail will now follow the bayou until mile 1.8, where the trail turns to the left (west) and crosses the bayou. The bayou is narrow and choked with brush in several places. It is possible to continue on across a short distance further to Mud Lake, but it will involve wading across the bayou much of the year. You can also continue to the right (east) a short distance on a rough path that leads to the edge of West Twin Lake. From the end of the trail, return the way you came to complete the out-and-back hike.

19 ▶ BIG CYPRESS TREE TRAIL

DISTANCE: 2.4 miles round-trip
TIME: 1 hour
DIFFICULTY: easy

DIRECTIONS: *This hike ends at the Arkansas state champion bald cypress tree. To reach the trailhead, enter the White River NWF at the Ethel entrance and immediately turn right (south) until you pass by Smokehouse Campground. At the first intersection, stay left and cross over Essex Bayou.*

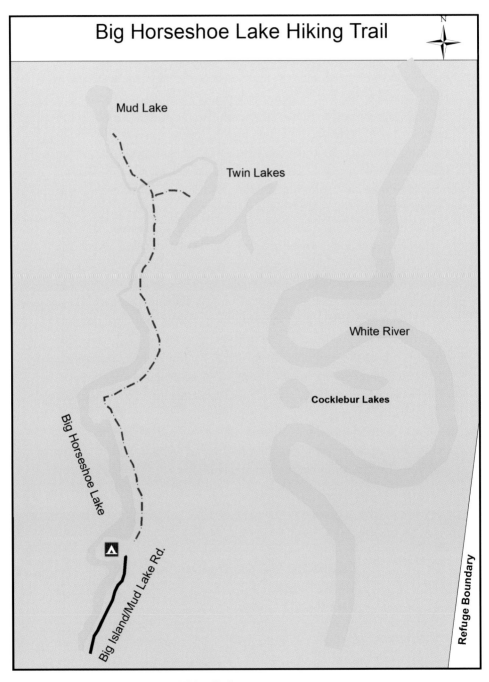

Big Horseshoe Lake Hiking Trail

Mud Lake

Twin Lakes

White River

Cocklebur Lakes

Big Horseshoe Lake

Big Island/Mud Lake Rd.

Refuge Boundary

FIGURE 82: Big Horseshoe Lake Hiking Trail.

Travel about one-half mile. The trailhead is on the left and is well marked with an interpretive sign (34.243448 N, 91.118075 W).

This delightful little trail (fig. 84) traverses through some high-quality bottomland forest before reaching a small bayou that contains the largest bald cypress (*Taxodium distichum*) in Arkansas, which also might be the largest living thing in the state (fig. 83). The trail has been improved with gravel and has several interpretive signs along the way explaining the plants and animals that can be found in this region. The forest along this trail has some old-growth characteristics, although extensive logging occurred in the past.

Several large specimens can be observed on the first mile of the trail. An excellent Nuttall's oak specimen is labeled. This common tree species of the Big Woods is one of the largest oak species in North America. Impressive overcup oaks can also be seen in this section of trail. With the many large, mature trees and large amount of standing dead timber, woodpeckers abound and can be seen and heard throughout.

After about 1.0 mile, the trail splits although it is not very well marked. Take the left-hand branch a few hundred yards to the state champion bald cypress, which will be obvious. An interpretive sign and park bench is provided. The big tree is indeed an impressive specimen. It is 43 feet in circumference above the base, which is swollen to an even greater girth, and about 120 feet tall. There is a large central trunk and two smaller trunks flanking it, with all three being fused from about 40 feet down to the base. Very impressive knees surround the tree, some up to 10 feet tall. The tree is hollow and is likely used by denning female bears during the winter. In fact, bear claw marks can be frequently seen on the bark. The tree is estimated to be about one thousand years old, although the hollow interior prevents a direct age calculation through ring analysis.

Many large and old cypress trees have a somewhat ragged look, with many dead branches in their crown. This tree is surprisingly intact and still has a rather youthful appearance, indicating that it still grows at a fairly rapid rate. It is clearly one of the most impressive biological specimens in all of Arkansas and should not be missed.

The small unnamed creek in which this tree sits feeds into Lower White Lake. The creek itself contains some other impressive cypress

FIGURE 83: Looking up at the state champion bald cypress tree. White River NWR near Ethel.

specimens, although none even remotely as large as the state champion. There are several old stumps within the creek bed, testimony to other large specimens that once existed here. They were undoubtedly logged during the early part of the last century. As to why this one specimen was spared the ax, nobody knows the answer. But about one hundred years ago, someone decided that this tree would remain standing, much to our benefit today. One can only imagine what an impressive sight an entire stand of trees this size would be.

Heading back on the trail to the split, turn left and walk about one hundred yards to the edge of Lower White Lake. It is a very pretty lake and contains abundant bird life. Just to the north of the hiking trail an ATV road also provides access to areas north of the lake and can also be hiked.

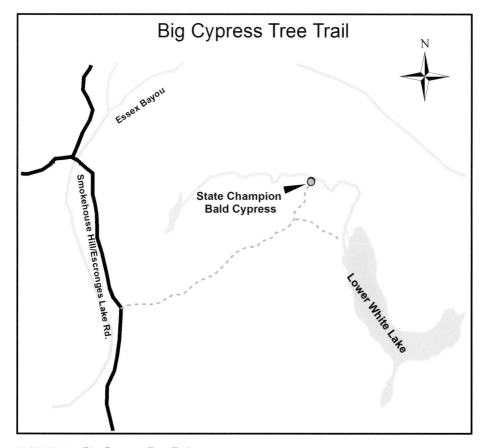

FIGURE 84: Big Cypress Tree Trail.

DISTANCE: 3.4 miles
TIME: 3–4 hours
DIFFICULTY: moderate with one short portage

DIRECTIONS: This canoe trail makes a loop around a popular lake in the White River NWR. One short portage may be necessary, depending upon water level. To reach the boat launch, enter at the Ethel entrance. Turn right, following signs to H-Lake, about 8.0 miles. A large primitive camping area is available at the end of the road, and an improved boat launch has been constructed (34.169920 N, 91.104307 W). The camping area can be crowded at times, and the lake is popular with fishermen. Wildlife viewing is good. An interpretive brochure describing this trail is available at the visitor center.

H-Lake provides an opportunity for a loop water trail, a rarity in canoe trails (fig. 85). The unusual shape of H-Lake, literally shaped like the letter "H," allows one to canoe the lower (southern) arms which are loosely connected by a narrow ditch. A short easy portage may be required during low water. The lake itself is extraordinarily pretty, and like most lakes in the area, very peaceful (see fig. 53). Wildlife viewing is consistently good, with many chances to spot waterfowl, upland birds, owls, deer, and small mammals. Bears are common and occasionally seen, although you are more likely to see signs of their presence (scratch marks, droppings, and tracks). A thin line of bald cypress trees lines the lake, while surrounding areas are made up mostly of bottomland forest dominated by overcup oak, sugarberry, and cherrybark oak. There are small areas of cypress-tupelo swamp in small depressions around the lake as well.

From the H-Lake Campground, turn right (south) down the southwest arm of the lake. The first section is wide-open water, but at 0.4 miles the lake forms a narrow channel. This sinuous section of the lake is quite pretty and contains several large cypress in the middle of the channel. At 0.8 miles the waterway opens up again into another open-water area. This section of the lake is a T-shaped portion of the lake that forms the far corner of the southwest branch of H-Lake, and

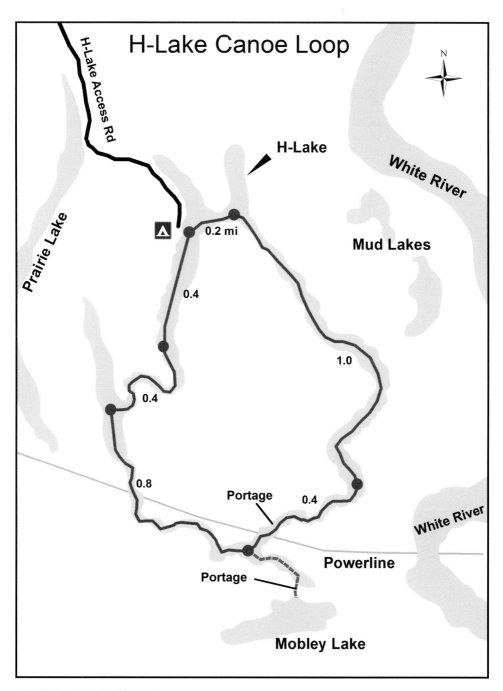

FIGURE 85: H-Lake Canoe Loop.

is referred to as Little H-Lake on most maps. Once in Little H-Lake, turn left (south). At the 1.1 mile mark, the lake turns east and narrows once again. This narrow bayou crosses a power line and then parallels it for a few hundred yards. This section of the lake is very picturesque. At 1.6 miles, the narrow section opens up into a small round pond that contains several nice cypress trees, including a large one with an incredible number of knees protruding from the water. To continue the loop, turn left (north) to where this small pond overlaps the power line right-of-way.

For an interesting side trip, it is possible to portage to Lake Mobley, just to the south. From the small pond, follow the lake to the east a few hundred yards until it peters out. From here, haul out your canoe and travel due south. The lake should be visible as soon as you reach the high ground on the south side of H-Lake. Lake Mobley is a medium-sized lake with no direct contact with other bodies of water in the White River NWR, although floodwaters from the White River spill into it during high water. There is an ATV trail that begins at H-Lake Campground and ends at Lake Mobley, and fisherman occasionally bring in their flat-bottomed boats. However, most of the time you will be canoeing Lake Mobley in solitude.

Back to H-Lake, there is a narrow ditch that connects from the power line right-of-way to the southeast arm of the lake (34.155221 N, 91.100160 W). During low water, a short, easy portage is necessary. During higher water, it is possible to follow the ditch, although over-hanging vegetation makes this route unpleasant. Once in the southeast arm (mile 1.7), continue paddling north. The southeast arm is some-what winding, but it is not as beautiful as the southwest arm. After traveling to mile 3.0, a small connector will appear to the west (left). The southeast arm of the lake narrows considerably just before this connector along a particularly pretty section. From here, one can see the boat launch, and it is short canoe ride back to the starting point, completing the loop (3.4 miles).

WHITE RIVER NWR: SOUTHEAST CORNER

One of the most remote regions of the Big Woods, and great place for viewing wildlife is the southeast corner of the White River NWR. Reached by driving many miles of dirt roads through fields and across levees, the long trip is well worth the effort (fig. 86). Wildlife viewing can be spectacular, and some of the prettiest forest is found in this section. Since the drive is so long, the best way to experience this section is to camp at the various sites established by the refuge. You must be self-sufficient as the nearest supplies are 20.0 miles away at Mellwood. There are great opportunities for canoeing and cross-country hiking in your search for wildlife. Two sites are described in this section, but cross-country hiking almost anywhere in this area would be rewarding. The Levee Loop Road traverses excellent areas of forest and provides access to many lakes in the region.

To reach the southeast corner of the Refuge, travel east from St. Charles over the Route 1 bridge, which crosses the White River, and continue for 10.0 miles. Turn right on Route 316 north and travel 3.5 miles. Turn right (south) on Route 318 and go 10.0 miles. Turn left (east) on Route 20 and travel 6.0 miles to the small town of Elaine. Turn right (south) on Route 44 and go 9.5 miles to Mellwood. The Mellwood Grocery on the left is a classic country store and the last stop for supplies. Turn right (west) onto County Road 518, where a refuge sign is located. This road is gravel but usually passable in any weather, but beware after heavy rains. Follow County Road 518 for 7.0 miles and emerge on top of the levee. Turn left (south) and drive atop the levee for 10.0 miles. Turn right (east) onto Levee Loop Road, which is the entrance to the refuge (34.090550 N, 91.062734 W).

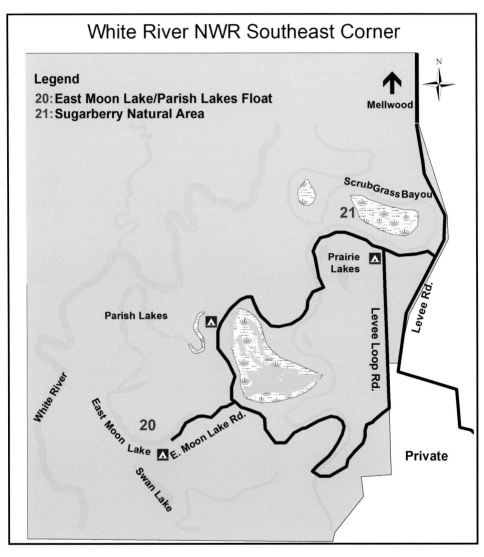

FIGURE 86: Southeast corner of the White River NWR with locations for trailheads.

DISTANCE: 11.6 miles round-trip
TIME: 8–10 hours
DIFFICULTY: moderate to difficult

DIRECTIONS: This full-day canoe trail traverses several interconnected lakes in the southeast portion of the refuge, one of the wildest and most wildlife-rich areas in all of the Big Woods. It is quite a journey to reach this remote section of the Big Woods and involves driving over many miles of gravel roads. To reach East Moon Lake (fig. 87) from Levee Loop Road, turn off the levee at the refuge entrance and travel for 1.0 mile to Campground S. Turn left (south) and follow the loop road for 7.3 miles. Turn left (east) at the sign for East Moon Lake. Follow the road for 1.5 miles until a small parking area appears along the lakeside at the primitive campground (34.043992 N, 91.153117 W). There is a boat launch available at the campground. If it is windy, this is a difficult float. A shorter float can be taken by turning around at any point desired.

This long float trip passes through several lakes in some of the most remote portions of the Big Woods (fig. 88). Wildlife is abundant, and

FIGURE 87: East Moon Lake. White River NWR.

there is a real chance for solitude. Much of the forest surrounding this float is minimally managed, and therefore, shows only minor signs of human activity. Start this canoe trip at the boat launch at East Moon Lake Campground. East Moon Lake is a large oxbow formed by a former path of the White River. Once in the lake, turn left (west) and paddle down this wide-open water. Do not paddle into the small bay that appears almost immediately on the left. Continue straight ahead into open water. There is a short section through some cypress trees at mile 0.4 after which the route goes back into open water. It is clear that this was once a deep river channel. The banks rise rather steeply into areas of high-quality bottomland forest typical of this region. The lake has a smattering of cypress lining it, although not nearly as many as are found in the more northern sections of the Big Woods. The forest to the left (west) of the lake is the Mink Bayou Natural Area, a three-thousand-acre section of forest that has not been logged in many years and is being minimally managed. You can beach the canoe at any time and explore this area on foot. After paddling for about 1.7 miles, two small offshoots appear on either side of the lake that extend a short distance. Continue straight ahead as the lake bends to the right (northeast). Just after the sharp bend at 2.0 miles, turn left into a small channel, which connects East Moon to the Parish Lakes region (34.057449 N, 91.169766 W).

The side channel is narrow but deep and easily navigable for some distance. At 2.8 miles, it then becomes shallower as it makes a sharp turn to the left (northwest). As it becomes shallower, numerous black willow trees emerge from the shallow water forming almost pure stands. This area is an excellent spot for seeing wildlife. Wood ducks are numerous in the flooded timber, and beaver activity is high. Willows are the favorite food of beavers, so it is not surprising that these animals are abundant here. Several beaver lodges can be seen in the flooded timber. The channel becomes even shallower and completely choked with willow before it enters Lower Parish Lake at the 3.4 mile mark. Navigating the last one hundred yards though the willows is a bit difficult and perhaps impassable during low water. Stay all the way to the left for the easiest pathway into Lower Parish Lake. Lower Parish has a round shape and a definite east-to-west depth gradient. To the east, the lake is very shallow with willow thickets lining the edge for several hundred feet. To the west, the lake is deeper and ends abruptly at good stands of bottomland forest.

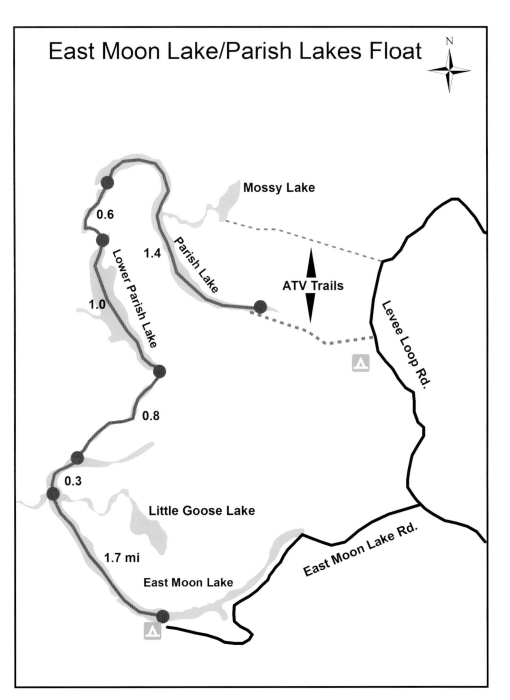

FIGURE 88: East Moon Lake/Parish Lakes Float.

The Parish Lakes region is a secluded area, and you are not likely to see other people in the area, although fishermen use the lake.

Travel north to where the lake narrows to a moderately large channel (3.8 mile mark) that connects to Parish Lake (4.4 mile mark). Parish Lake is a fairly wide and long lake similar to East Moon. As the lake first widens, a narrow chute appears to the left (west) but is entirely willow choked and not navigable under normal water levels. Parish Lake then bends to make a 180-degree turn. At the outside bend of this turn at the 4.8 mile mark is a small ditch (known as a blowout) that connects the lake to the White River (34.085507 N, 91.160219 W). According to locals familiar with the area, this blowout occurred recently as flood water receded from Parish Lake back into the White River. In recent years the White River NWR personnel have constructed stabilizing structures around the ditch to prevent further erosion and draining of the lake. For an easy look at the White River, pull the canoe into the small ditch, walk about two hundred feet to the west, and observe the power of the river. It appears to be rather rapidly cutting into the bank so that in the not-too-distant future it will spill into Parish Lake. What kind of changes will occur at that point is only conjecture but shows the potential of the large bottomland rivers to change course dramatically at times.

Back in the canoe, continue up Parish Lake. A small opening appears on the left bank at the 5.1 mile mark that connects to several other small lakes (Mossy and Long Lakes), but the author has not explored the area. After traveling another mile to the southeast, the lake narrows down to an impassable channel at mile 5.8. Turn around and retrace your path back to East Moon Lake campground. If time permits, an exploration of some of the side channels in East Moon and the Parish Lakes would probably be rewarding, but it is a long trip back to the launch site. If you have an ATV, it is possible to drag a canoe from the end point of the canoe trail to Campground T (an ATV trail is available on the east side of Parish Lake; turn left once out of the lake and on the trail). If you do not have a boat, the ATV trail to Parish Lake and another one that goes to Mossy Lake make good hiking trails.

No trail: wander at will
DIFFICULTY: easy

DIRECTIONS: The Sugarberry Natural Area is perhaps the largest section of old-growth bottomland forest in the Big Woods region (fig. 89). It is a small example of what once covered millions of acres of eastern Arkansas. To reach the site, park at Campground S (fig. 22, 34.094108 N, 91.079569 W)). Just to the north is Scrubgrass Bayou. Campground S is 1.0 mile after the turnoff from the levee (see directions in previous section). In a small boat or canoe, cross the bayou, which is about fifty yards wide. Beach the boat on the following side, and you enter a magnificent stand of trees. It might be possible to cross Scrubgrass Bayou on foot during extremely dry periods, but that prospect is unlikely.

At the time of European settlement, much of eastern Arkansas was covered with impressive stands of bottomland forest. Sadly, most of that is gone, converted to agriculture or cut over multiple times for America's insatiable appetite for wood. The Sugarberry Natural Area (fig. 90) represents one small surviving piece of what once was. The trees are indeed impressive with several large specimens and at least one state champion species. What is also noticeable is the difference in structure of this forest. It simply looks different from the other areas of the Big Woods, which may contain very nice stands of forest, but none that compare to an uncut forest. The dominant tree species at this site are Nuttall's oak, overcup oak, sweet pecan, and green ash (*Fraxinus pennsylvanica*). Large numbers of sugarberry, as expected by the area's name, are also present, although this tree species does not get particularly large.

Other characteristics of this forest are readily evident. Many areas of the Big Woods are made up of even-aged stands of trees that have sprouted since the last timber harvest occurred. Since many areas have not been cut in over eighty years, a majestic forest has grown. But at Sugarberry, the trees are uneven in age. There are many rotund giants, but also many medium-sized trees, and many young trees as well. Numerous standing dead trees (known as snags) also populate the forest, and many huge logs litter the ground, slowly decomposing. The

snags and downed trees are incredibly important to many animals of the forest as they provide homes and food for many different species. The forest looks much more chaotic as well, chaos that is probably more properly referred to as complexity.

Besides the impressive trees, numerous large vines, probably of great age, also drape across the forest. Huge grape vine, poison ivy, and other species add more complexity. One must experience this type of forest to understand its grandeur, which makes this place a must-see location in the Big Woods.

There are no trails in the Sugarberry, but it is quite easy to walk where you please. Scrubgrass Bayou makes a long lazy bend, traveling to the east almost to the refuge boundary before looping around to the west, almost touching the east-bound part of the bayou. The central part of the land area is mostly open swamp with very few trees, while the higher land along the inside edge of Scrubgrass Bayou contains most of the old-growth forest. The "teardrop" just to the northwest of the main site is also believed to be uncut forest, but a long canoe ride would be necessary to reach it from the Campground S launching site. You could, however, try a portage where Levee Loop Road comes very close to the site (fig. 24, 34.097813 N, 91.098933 W).

THE CONFLUENCE

The area below the White River NWR is where the three great rivers, the White, the Arkansas, and the Mississippi, merge in a tangle of water and woods. Much of the area is difficult to access, and most of the property is privately owned by timber companies and hunting lodges. There are a few public areas, however, that will reward the interested explorer and adventuresome traveler. The last section of the Arkansas River is a wild river experience that harkens back to pre-settlement days. Most of the area is remote, and services are limited.

The White River NWR is hoping to expand their land holdings into this region. If the acquisition boundary expansion proposal is approved, it will buy land from willing landowners. These purchases will help

FIGURE 89: Old-growth forest in the Sugarberry Natural Area. White River NWR.

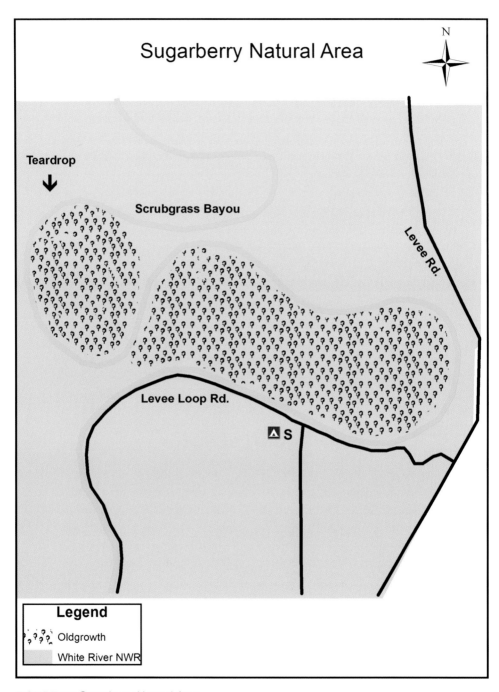

FIGURE 90: Sugarberry Natural Area.

protect a very important section of bottomland forest as well as the lonely free-flowing section of the lower Arkansas River.

Arkansas Post National Memorial

To reach the park, travel south on Route 165/1 from DeWitt for 18.0 miles. Turn left (east) onto Route 169 and travel for 1.5 miles, where the road crosses Little Post Bayou. Good wildlife viewing, including alligators, is often available at the bridge. Continue for another 0.5 miles. Turn right (south) onto Old Post Road and go 1.0 mile to the visitor center (34.016680 N, 91.345198 W). The route is well signed.

The only National Park Service site in the Big Woods commemorates the first European settlement in Arkansas. Although mostly a historical site—and a fascinating history indeed—it also has some great wildlife-viewing opportunities. There is not much impressive forest here since it is recent regrowth and most of the park is maintained as open fields for historical purposes. The extensive wetland areas around Arkansas Post, however, are particularly good for viewing aquatic wildlife. White-tailed deer are extremely common in the park's open area, and they are habituated to human presence, so you should get excellent views of them. The park is also great for those who do not want to "rough it." Several of the trails are handicapped accessible, and the park even has a family nature pack that includes field guides and binoculars. For those with mobility issues, you can rent a wheelchair. Digital cameras are also available for rent.

23 ➤ POST BAYOU NATURE TRAIL

DISTANCE: 1.3 miles
TIME: .5–1 hour
DIFFICULTY: easy; parts are handicapped accessible

DIRECTIONS: This trail (fig. 91) makes a short loop through fields, forest, and along Post Bayou (fig. 93).

FIGURE 91: Post Bayou Nature Trail. Arkansas Post National Memorial.

Begin at the parking lot in front of the visitor center and walk along the entrance road to the park. Just to your left at 0.1 miles is the state champion Osage orange tree (*Maclura pomifera*), also known as bois d'arc, which is labeled with a plaque (fig. 92). This unusual tree, not related to citrus plants (it is actually in the mulberry family), produces a large green fruit in the autumn that can contain hundreds of seeds. The tree is famous for producing the preferred wood for Native American bows as it is extremely strong and flexible (Keeler, 1900).

Just past the Osage orange tree, take the paved trail to the left. Follow this trail to the west through open fields, passing several interpretive signs about the history of the site. At a four-way junction, go straight and head toward the Post Bayou. Just before reaching the bayou, the trail enters a wooded area of upland forest. Arkansas Post was established at this location because of the relatively high ground, which is part of the Grand Prairie Terrace, and does not usually flood. White oak, mockernut hickory, and eastern red cedar are common tree species. As you reach the bayou (0.25 miles), you will notice specimens of dwarf palmetto (*Sabel minor*), the only species of palm found in

FIGURE 92: State champion Osage orange (*Maclura pomifera*). Arkansas Post National Memorial. Courtesy of Heather McPherson.

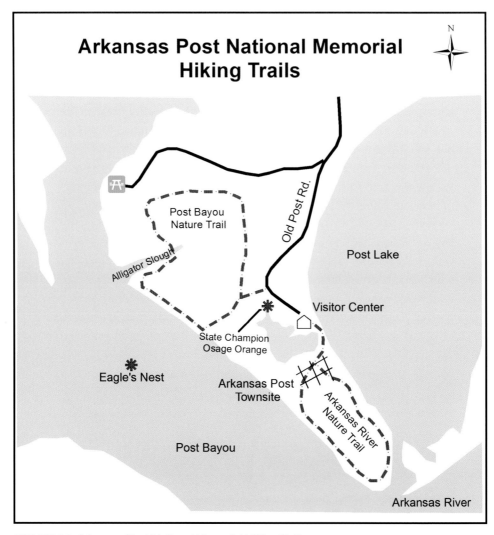

FIGURE 93: Arkansas Post National Memorial Hiking Trails.

Arkansas, which reaches its northern limit near Arkansas Post. The trail follows the Post Bayou for 0.2 miles. Across the bayou note the large nest in one of the submerged cypress trees. It is a resident bald eagle nest, and often the eagles will be seen in attendance, especially during breeding season from February through May. During the warmer months, this part of the trail is a place to be on the lookout for alligators. Arkansas Post is probably the most reliable place to see them as they have abundant aquatic habitat next to rarely flooded high ground, necessary for breeding and hibernation. The best place to see them is around the bridge over Little Post Bayou as you enter the park, but any body of water is a possibility for a sighting. Some large specimens over ten feet long are present.

The trail then turns right, parallels Alligator Slough, then a small bridge crosses it at the 0.6 mile mark. This body of water is very small and not likely to contain many alligators for which it is named. From here the trail winds away from the bayou and into the forest, and it passes a few grassland areas as well. After a few hundred yards, there is a left turnoff to the picnic area. Continue straight on the trail that passes through young upland forest. In this area are the remains of a Civil War battle that occurred here, and rifle pits and trenches can still be seen. At 1.0 miles, turn right onto the connector trail, which returns to the open field and completes the trail.

24 ➤ ARKANSAS RIVER NATURE TRAIL

DISTANCE: 1 miles
TIME: 30 minutes
DIFFICULTY: easy

DIRECTIONS: This short trail provides an overlook of Post Bend, Post Bayou, and the Arkansas River (fig. 93). Start from behind the visitor center.

From the visitor center follow one of several paths through the old town site of Arkansas Post for about 0.25 miles. Go to the far right and follow the path along the shoreline of Post Bayou. At the 0.5 mile mark, the trail reaches the Arkansas River overlook, where there are several benches. From this point, you can see the Arkansas River straight ahead, Post Bayou to your right, and Post Bend to your left (fig. 94). Typically there are a lot of waterfowl to be observed, and by sitting quietly you will likely see many species. Along the banks of Post Bend and Post Bayou, you will also see large mats of vegetation covered with very pretty purple flowers in summer. Unfortunately this plant is the invasive water hyacinth (*Eichhornia crassipes*), one of the most destructive introduced species in North America (fig. 95). Originally found in

FIGURE 94: View from Arkansas River Nature Trail. Arkansas Post National Memorial.

the Amazon Basin, it has been introduced around the world with disastrous consequences (Penfield and Earle, 1948). It grows extremely rapidly and densely, and can even prevent the passage of boat traffic. Because of its rapid growth, it can out compete native vegetation and have negative impacts on native aquatic animals. At the moment, the Big Woods has limited areas where it has been established, mostly in the southern area along backwater areas of the lower Arkansas River, but it is a severe threat to all of

FIGURE 95: Water hyacinth (*E. crassipes*).

the Big Woods. It does not survive well in moving water, so the major free flowing rivers seem fairly immune, but the numerous lakes in the Big Woods that are important for wildlife are at risk. Unfortunately, the plant is popular with some ornamental pond enthusiasts who have undoubtedly increased its range. It should never be transported to any body of water (including backyard ornamental ponds), and its sale in Arkansas is illegal.

Continue following the trail around the opposite side of the peninsula until it emerges back at the old townsite (0.8 miles). From there follow one of the various trails through the town site back to the visitor center to complete the trail.

25 ➤ ARKANSAS POST WATER TRAIL

DISTANCE: 4.6 miles
TIME: 3 hours
DIFFICULTY: moderate

DIRECTIONS: From the Route 165/1 intersection with Route 169, follow Route 169 east for 0.8 miles. Turn right into a small parking area. A boat launch is available (34.025549 N, 91.362451 W). Because of the water hyacinth growth, the trail is only passable in winter and spring.

This official state water trail (fig. 98) passes through several bodies of water around Arkansas Post National Memorial and Trusten Holder WMA (fig. 96), and is a good place to spot American alligators (fig.

FIGURE 96: Post Lake, part of the Arkansas Post Water Trail. Trusten Holder WMA and Arkansas Post National Memorial.

39). Caution should be exercised in the open water areas on this trail during high winds. From the launch you can proceed either right or left. To the right is the narrow confines of Moore Bayou. I have not yet been able to traverse this section because of dense water hyacinth growth (see previous section for a description of this insidious species). To the left, follow Moore Bayou downstream. The initial parts of the trail pass through a narrow section of the bayou that is surrounded by young bottomland forest. After 0.5 miles, a left turn heads up Little Post Bayou, which can be followed for some distance depending on the water hyacinth density. Just past the Route 169 Bridge, all lands surrounding the bayou are private. Turn right at the junction with Little Post Bayou, and you will soon emerge into Post Bayou (0.6 mile mark), which is a large wide-open body of water. The area around the junction of Moore Creek, Little Post Bayou, and Post Bayou is one of the premier places to see alligators. Waterfowl also abound, and you are likely to see great egrets, great blue herons, and a variety of ducks. In the distance on the southwest side of the Post Bayou the bald eagle nest is clearly visible.

Paddle along the east side of the bayou staying close to the shore-line, which is part of Arkansas Post National Memorial. It is not permitted to land a canoe anywhere on the National Park land, so stay in the water. Water hyacinth is common here, forming large mats. Interspersed is also a good population of American lotus flower (*Nelumbo lutea*), a native species. This aquatic plant produces beautiful white flowers in summer and then unusually shaped seed pods in fall (fig. 97). It is likely that this native species is being reduced by the spread of the water hyacinth. There are a few scattered cypress trees in the bayou that are good perching spots for a variety of birds especially double-crested cormorants (*Phalacrocorax auritus*), which are common throughout the year. Follow the shoreline until you come to a point (1.7 mile mark), which is the lookout spot for the Arkansas River Nature Trail described in the previous section. To your right is the Arkansas River, which you want to avoid because of the strong currents usually present.

Round the point and you will enter Post Lake. Post Lake is very similar to Post Bayou with similar birdlife. It is a bit more sheltered and seems to have more ducks present in winter. Beavers are also common in Post Lake and allow unusually close approach, offering some very good views of their complex behaviors. The trail officially ends adjacent

FIGURE 97: Lotus flower (*Nelumbo nucifera*) with its unusual fruit.

to the visitor center at mile 2.3. From Post Lake, retrace your route back to the parking area.

Trusten Holder WMA

The Trusten Holder WMA protects tracts of land along the lower sections of the White and Arkansas Rivers (fig. 99). It is jointly managed by the Arkansas Game and Fish Commission and the Army Corps of Engineers. It is primarily used by hunters but provides excellent wildlife viewing. The various trails that are maintained for hunters can also be utilized by hikers seeking wildlife-viewing opportunities. The wildlife management area is divided into three areas. Area 1 includes the lands just south of the White River NWR along the south side of the Arkansas Post Canal. There is excellent bird watching in this area and also one of the better places in the Big Woods for black bear sightings. If you decide to camp in the area, be particularly cautious with food to avoid unwanted bear attention. Area 2 protects lands between State Route 165 and the Pendleton Dam, including most of the land and water that surrounds the Arkansas Post National Memorial. Area 2 has good opportunities for seeing waterfowl and other water-loving birds.

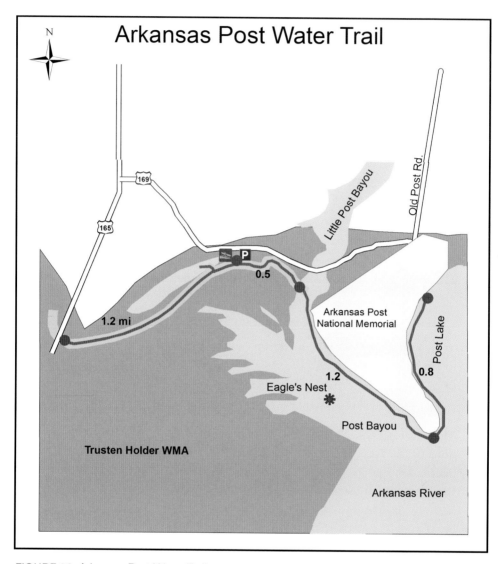

FIGURE 98: Arkansas Post Water Trail.

Area 3 surrounds Lake Merrisach, a popular fishing lake and good place
to see waterfowl. Visiting parts of Trusten Holder sometimes involves
long drives, although roads tend to be in good condition. Even though
it appears possible on a map, no cars can cross the Pendleton Dam to
get from one side of the river to the other. You have to drive around and
cross over Route 165/1.

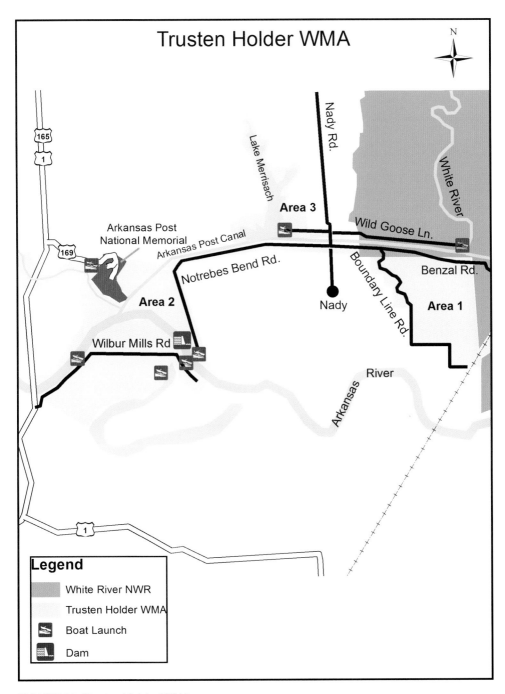

FIGURE 99: Trusten Holder WMA.

DISTANCE: 6.6 miles round-trip
TIME: 4 hours
DIFFICULTY: easy but rather long; moderate after rains

DIRECTIONS: This trail traverses bottomland forests and has good wild-life-viewing opportunities. From DeWitt, travel south on Route 165 for 8.0 miles. Turn left (east) on Route 44 to the town of Tichnor, which is 5.0 miles distant. After passing through town, go straight onto Tichnor Blacktop Road (do not stay on Route 44). After 5.0 miles, the road comes to a T; turn left. The road turns right again almost immediately. Follow for another 2.5 miles until you cross over the Arkansas Post Canal. Immediately after crossing the canal, turn left (east) onto Benzal Road, a gravel road, which parallels the canal. Travel 1.3 miles and turn (south) right into a small primitive campground (34.022652 N, 91.224319 W). This road is passable by all vehicles but does sometimes flood. Follow the road for 2.1 miles until you come to the Handicapped Access trail on the left (34.000771 N, 91.212649 W). If you have two cars for a shuttle, follow Benzal Road from the campground turnoff for another 4.3 miles. Just before the Yancopin Railroad Bridge, there is a small parking area, which is the east terminus of the trail (34.004472 N, 91.163559 W). During deer-hunting season, the trail is used by mobility-impaired hunters and should not be visited. The rest of the year, it is a great trail for wildlife watching.

This trail travels from west to east across a pleasant section of Area 1 of the Trusten Holder WMA (fig. 100). The trail can be muddy after rains but is generally passable unless the major rivers in the area flood. Much of the land along the trail was thinned around 2010, which makes the area somewhat less aesthetically pleasing, but also makes wildlife viewing easier. When entering from the west side, the forest is dominated by extensive stands of sugarberry trees, while the more typical oaks and hickories are noticeably scarce. During winter, extraordinary numbers of berry-loving birds often descend upon the area to feed on the fruit of these trees. American robins, cedar waxwings, and

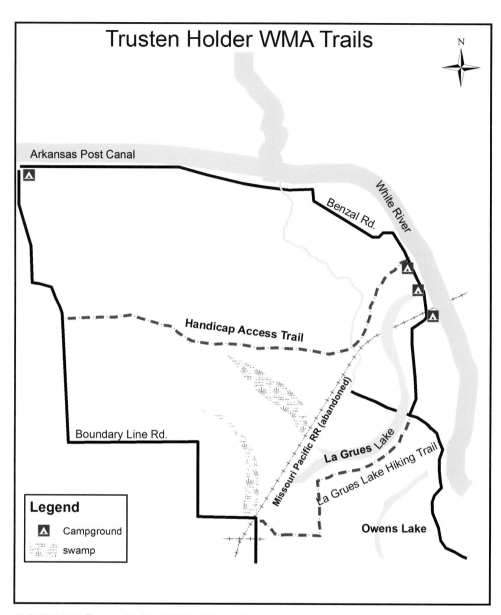

Trusten Holder WMA Trails

N

Arkansas Post Canal

White River

Benzal Rd.

Handicap Access Trail

Boundary Line Rd.

Missouri Pacific RR (abandoned)

La Grues Lake

La Grues Lake Hiking Trail

Owens Lake

Legend

△ Campground

⸏⸏ swamp

FIGURE 100: Trusten Holder WMA hiking trails.

grackles are often seen in large flocks foraging in the area, and there is a good chance to see a flock of the increasingly rare rusty blackbirds. The trail passes through this type of forest for about 1.3 miles, where a swamp appears on the south (right) side of the trail. In the vicinity of this swampy area, several side trails branch off both north and south of the Handicapped Trail. The ones to the south are often flooded except during dry periods. The one to the north is usually passable. Some of these can be combined with the Handicapped Trail to form loop trails (See Trusten Holder website, appendix 2). A few impressive bald cypress are present, and wood ducks are common. After this point, the vegetation changes somewhat, and there are larger numbers of oaks. This more diverse forest supports a higher diversity of birds and also tends to produce good deer sightings. The trail also gets a bit muddy as you travel east. At 2.5 miles, the trail passes over a small creek. Usually you can hop over it without getting wet. Just before this creek, the trail actually passes into the White River NWR, which owns some of the land in the area. The Yancopin Bridge, part of an old railway line, appears on the right. The rest of the trail follows through more typical oak-hickory forest until it ends at Benzal Road (mile 3.3). If you do not have a shuttle, return the way you came.

27 ➤ LAGRUES LAKE HIKING TRAIL (UNOFFICIAL)

DISTANCE: 2.5 miles round-trip
TIME: 1.5 hours
DIFFICULTY: easy

DIRECTIONS: To reach this trail, follow Benzal Road 6.0 miles from the canal bridge until it passes under the railroad. After this point, the road travels along the east side of the lake. Follow for another 0.9 miles. A small parking area will appear just before the road makes a sharp left turn (33.986502 N, 91.165168 W).

The trail begins at a water-control structure that crosses LaGrues Lake (fig. 100). The rocks that cover this dike often contain several species of snakes sunning themselves in the morning. Cottonmouths are common, so caution is advised, although most of what you see will be nonvenomous water snakes (*Nerodia*). Follow the trail into the woods as it parallels the lake. In the first section of the trail, the forest has been thinned in recent years. For the first 0.9 miles of the trail, the lake is easily visible, and good views of waterfowl are likely. A small swamp to the left also contains waterfowl at times. The forest in this section is an oak–sweet pecan–sugarberry type and is an excellent wildlife habitat. Bears appear to use the area frequently, and their sign is often seen. At mile 1.0, the trail makes a sharp left turn. On the right is a forest that has not been harvested in many years and is very open along the ground. The trail is now following the boundary between the White River NWR on the right and the Trusten Holder WMA on the left. After another 0.25 miles, the trail makes a sharp right turn and then soon after another sharp right. Soon you will approach the railroad tracks. The forest in this region is very pretty, and visibility is good during the winter as the understory is quite open.

You can continue on past the railroad tracks for some distance, although the trail becomes very swampy at times. Return the way you came back to the trailhead.

FIGURE 101: A red-cockcaded woodpecker (*Picoides borealis*) on a large pine.

Sites Outside
of the Big Woods

Outside the contiguous Big Woods, there are additional isolated areas that harbor interesting habitats and species, including some that are endangered.

28 ➤ PINE CITY NATURAL AREA/
RED-COCKADED WOODPECKER SITE
ARKANSAS NATURAL HERITAGE COMMISSION

DIRECTIONS: From Clarendon, take Route 79 east about 5.0 miles to Route 17. Turn right and go south on Route 17 approximately 6.0 miles to Route 86. Turn left (east) on Route 86 for 3.0 miles. There are several areas of land owned by the Arkansas Natural Heritage Commission, some in various stages of regeneration. The best site to visit is on the right and contains a nice stand of mature pines. A small parking area that can hold about two cars is located just before the preserve sign (34.603569 N, 91.123322 W). This site contains a federally protected population of red-cockaded woodpeckers (Picoides borealis, fig. 101), and visitors should refrain from disturbing them. Please view them from a respectable distance.

Pine City contains a "lost" population of loblolly pines (*Pinus taeda*) surrounded by the great bottomland forests (although mostly cleared for agriculture today) of the Arkansas Delta. Loblolly pine is very common farther to the south in Arkansas and across the Gulf and Atlantic

177

Coasts. Because of unusual landforms located at this site that drain quickly, pines dominate the landscape instead of the usual oak-hickory bottomland forests that characterize the Delta (Bragg, 2005). The pines have apparently been isolated here for some time, and they represent a genetically distinct variety found nowhere else in the United States (Rupar and Warriner, 2009). The Arkansas Heritage Commission is working to propagate the variety and is encouraging local landowners to replant.

There is no real trail through the site, and to minimize disturbance to the red-cockaded woodpecker's habitat, do not travel very far into the preserve. From the parking area, walk a few hundred yards to the east (left), listen carefully, and watch the treetops. The woodpeckers are usually easy to find as they noisily forage in the treetops, usually near the artificial nest boxes that have been constructed in some of the pines. I have seen them every time I have visited the site.

Red-cockaded woodpeckers are distinguished from other local woodpeckers by the large white cheek patch and uniformly dark cap on their heads (fig. 101). They often forage with other more common woodpeckers. This endangered species requires old-growth pines (mostly loblolly pine or longleaf pine), and is unusual in that it excavates nest cavities in living trees. The woodpeckers prefer old trees that have become infected with fungus known as red heart rot, which softens the heart wood. Even when a tree is infected, the woodpeckers still require at least two years to excavate a nest cavity. Once a nest cavity has been created, the woodpeckers open small holes in the tree below the nest, from which sap flows. The sap presumably helps deter predators from entering the nest (Walters, 1991). Red-cockaded woodpeckers are also unusual in that they exhibit cooperative breeding, with the nesting pair assisted by juvenile helpers, usually male offspring of the breeding pair (Walters et al., 1988).

The Arkansas Heritage Commission has assisted the birds by install-ing artificial nesting cavities constructed in the large pine trees. The birds readily utilize these structures, several of which can be seen near the road. The preserve is also burned periodically to remove under-growth, as the birds prefer more open parklike habitat. This popula-tion of red-cockaded woodpeckers is the last surviving group in the Arkansas Delta.

DIRECTIONS: This small state park preserves an important historic site related to the settlement of the United States and also protects a headwater swamp. From Clarendon, take Route 79 east for about 10.0 miles to the junction with Route 49. Turn right on Route 49 south and follow for 8.0 miles. Turn left (east) onto Route 362, where there is a sign clearly marking the park. Follow this road for about 2.0 miles until it dead ends at the small parking area (34.645721 N, 91.054010 W). The boardwalk is handicapped accessible.

The charming little state park protects a habitat known as a headwater swamp, a habitat that is very rare in Arkansas today (fig. 102). Headwater swamps are depressions that gather water from nearby high areas and tend to remain flooded most of the year. Unlike in the rivers and creeks in the area, there is no current, and these habitats provide

FIGURE 102: Headwater swamp with almost pure stand of water tupelo (*Nyassa aquatic*). Louisiana Purchase State Park.

important breeding areas for many aquatic organisms. The two most common trees are water tupelo and bald cypress. This site is the best place to access a tupelo-cypress swamp without a boat. In Arkansas headwater swamps occur only in a narrow belt in the southeast portion of the state between the towns of Marianna and Clarendon. Most were ditched and drained for agriculture many years ago. This state park preserves one of the best examples left.

A short boardwalk provides year-round access to the swamp and has interpretive signs. The tupelo-cypress forest appears quite young and was undoubtedly harvested in the past. It has grown back quite nicely, though, and the hydrology of the site is still mostly intact with few signs of ditching. Amphibian numbers are very high in the spring, and as one of the interpretive signs indicate, the rare bird-voiced tree frog (*Hyla avivoca*) breeds here. This very pretty species of tree frog can be found breeding in April or May, depending on the weather patterns. The rest of the year it lives high in the trees and is unlikely to be seen. Bird life is fairly prolific, and by sitting quietly on the benches provided, you are likely to see several species.

When you reach the end of the boardwalk, a large stone monument has been placed. It was at this point from which almost all the land in the Louisiana Purchase was surveyed. Basically all property lines west of the Mississippi were set from this inauspicious point. One can only imagine how remote this site must have been in 1815 when the surveyors established the point.

30 ▶ RAILROAD PRAIRIE AND DOWNS PRAIRIE NATURAL AREAS

DIRECTIONS: To reach these two small prairie preserves, exit Interstate 40 at the Carlisle Exit (exit 183) and turn south onto Route. 13. Travel for 1.3 miles to downtown Carlisle. Turn left (east) onto Route 70. Travel 1.3 miles and the Railroad Prairie will appear on the left (north) side of the road (34.782005 N, 91.706750 W). The prairie extends for about 6.0 miles until you come to the small town of Hazen. Continue traveling east for another 3.2 miles, and the prairie will reappear on the north side of the road and extend for another two miles. At the intersection of Route 70 and Lawman

FIGURE 103: Grasslands at Downs Prairie Natural Area.

Road (County Road 24), the Downs Prairie appears on both sides of the road (34.781563 N, 91.496760 W). The east end of the Railroad Prairie and the Downs Prairie are shown in fig. 104.

The Nature Conservancy and the Arkansas Natural Heritage Commission have been active for many years in attempting to preserve remnants of the grasslands throughout the state. Two of their holdings can be visited and are easily accessible along Route 70 (fig. 103). The Grand Prairie Terrace was once covered by extensive grasslands with attendant species such as bison, elk, and prairie chickens. Only 1 percent remains today, and although the big mammals and many grassland specialist birds are gone, the plants and smaller animals remain at these two tiny preserves. The dominant plants here are various grasses such as little bluestem (*Schizachyrium scoparium*), big bluestem (*Andropogon gerardii*), and Indian grass (*Sorghastrum nutans*). Pretty flowering plants can be seen throughout the warmer months of the year including several species of sunflowers (*Helianthus*), indigo (*Baptisia*), and butterfly weed (*Asclepias tuberosa*). The compass plant (*Silphium laciniatum*) with its tall flower stems with gorgeous yellow flowers can be seen in summer. The prairie mole cricket (*Gryllotalpa major*), now extremely rare in Arkansas, can be found at these two sites, although you are unlikely to see one since they live underground. You can walk freely throughout the preserves. Some of the best times are spring and fall when flowering plants are abundant.

From the east end of the Railroad Prairie (fig. 104), you can see

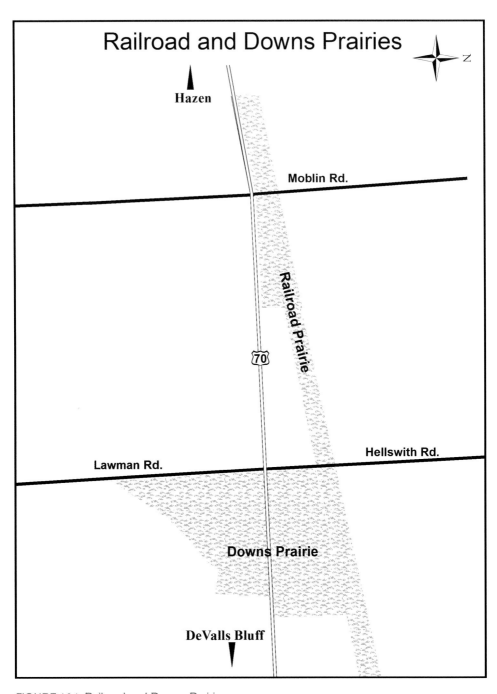

FIGURE 104: Railroad and Downs Prairies.

many miles to the south, almost to the horizon. Just 150 years ago, this view would have been across unbroken prairie. These two small preserves, plus a few even smaller ones around Stuttgart, are all that survive today. Visit the Arkansas Heritage Website (appendix 2) for more information on these interesting areas.

BIRDING ON THE GRAND PRAIRIE AND SURROUNDING LANDS

Most of the land on the Grand Prairie Terrace was converted to agriculture years ago. After the fields are harvested in the fall, the crop waste attracts huge numbers of waterfowl. Fields are often intentionally flooded or simply fill up with the winter rains, and they provide habitat for many species. As they dry out, the exposed mud often attracts good numbers of shorebirds. Other areas that remain dry throughout the year support upland birds. Fish farming has also become popular, and the artificial ponds attract many wading birds. With the immense number of birds feeding on the grain in the fields, predatory birds are not far behind. In winter, raptors become particularly abundant. The best strategy is to drive around on the roads until flocks of birds are located. Once they are found, be sure to pull well off the road wherever you can find a place to park. The numerous gravel roads throughout the region also provide access to many out-of-the-way areas. Driving almost anywhere in the region will yield plenty of birds, and I have described some of the best routes below.

ROUTE 165 BETWEEN STUTTGART AND DEWITT

One of the best areas for bird watching (fig. 74). Expect to see great numbers of snow geese, plenty of ducks, and big flocks of blackbirds.

ROUTE 33 BETWEEN DEVALLS BLUFF AND DEWITT

This road travels southeast and skirts the edge of the White River NWR, passing through many small communities along the way (fig. 74). Waterfowl are common throughout.

ROUTE 44 BETWEEN HELENA AND SLOW LAKE

This route, well east of the Grand Prairie, passes between the Mississippi River and the White River through a rather remote section of east Arkansas and, along the way, passes by Old Town Lake, a large oxbow of the Mississippi (fig. 74). Birding is excellent throughout. At Mellwood is the turnoff to the southeast corner of the White River Refuge described in a previous section. This access road tends to have many birds visible, especially as you approach the refuge boundary.

ROUTE 17 BETWEEN BRINKLEY AND PATTERSON

This rather lightly traveled road passes between Bayou DeView and the Cache River (fig. 55). Good birding is found throughout.

An Exploratory Trip down the Arkansas: A Cautionary Tale

What follows is an account of the attempted trip by the author down the final section of the lower Arkansas River in the fall of 2011.

The lower Arkansas River below the Pendleton Dam is a remnant of history and worthy of exploration. Because of engineering difficulties, the Army Corps decided not to channelize the lower twenty-nine miles of the river when they built the McClellan-Kerr navigational system in the early 1970s, but instead decided to build a canal (the Arkansas Post Canal) from Pendleton to the lower White River and then into the Mississippi (see fig. 98). Therefore, those last miles of the river represent the Arkansas River in is primitive state, a rarity on a river that large. Between Pendleton and the Mississippi, the river flows under its own direction. The lands surrounding it are wild, and although mostly privately held, they exist inside the levee constraints and in an almost wilderness state controlled not by humans, but the natural and unpredictable ebb and flow of the floods. Therefore, it was an obvious decision for me to try to explore the area for this book.

The plan was to launch just below the Pendleton Dam and travel down the Arkansas and into the mighty Mississippi. From there, we would take the boat down the "old man" about eighteen miles downstream to Arkansas City. There, the Choctaw Island WMA had boat launch where we would park our shuttle car. That was a total of forty-eight miles, and we only had about three days to do it, so the canoe was out of the question. Awesome I thought! We can take the bass boat. I am sure my wife Jennifer rolled her eyes when I mentioned it, but she was willing to go on another of my adventures. We would head downstream fairly slowly on the first day from Pendleton, camp overnight on the sandbars of the river, then reach the Mississippi the second day and run full speed down to Arkansas City to meet our waiting car. With an extra day to spare, it all seemed like a solid plan. It definitely was not.

November 10, 2011. The early morning drive from central Arkansas, down through Pine Bluff, through the small Delta towns of Dumas, Michellville, and McGehee went without incident, and we arrived at Arkansas City by midmorning. We dropped off the car, and with the bass boat in tow behind my pickup, we headed up to Pendleton to start our journey. We arrived about one-half hour later and launched the boat without incident. We loaded the boat with camping supplies, food, clothes, rain gear, a full fuel tank, plus an extra five gallons of gas just in case. The river was flowing strongly as we pushed off and headed down into the wild stretch of the great Arkansas River. The Pendleton Dam was open so the flow was strong, and we made good time heading downstream. The river was beautiful and we saw lots of wildlife: hundreds of herons, egrets, ospreys, and even an eagle. We also got our first look at the Asian flying carp we had heard so much about. Apparently, they had already colonized this section of the river, and we could occasionally see one leap away from the boat (and fortunately never into the boat, as they are known to do sometimes).

By late afternoon, we passed under the spectacular Yancopin Railroad Bridge and decided this would be a good place to camp (fig. 105). We pulled up on the north bank of the river where a broad plain of soft white sand greeted us. It was a perfect place to pitch a tent. I was aware of the possibility of rising and falling water (honestly most concerned about rising water), so I placed two anchors far up on the bank of the river and tied off the boat securely, double checking all my lines.

FIGURE 105: View of the Yancopin Bridge on the lower section of the Arkansas River.

The tent was pitched, dinner was some fresh snapper recently caught in the Gulf of Mexico, and we went off to sleep under a cloudless night with just the stars as our companions. All was well in our world, and we slept soundly until sunrise.

November 11, 2011. The next morning was chilly and I quickly got out of the tent to get some hot water started. It was then that I noticed a small problem. The boat was now far from the river. During the night, the river had fallen about fifteen feet. Clearly the dam had been closed and the water shut off. It was at that moment that I realized that I was not sure about the weight of my bass boat. I was pretty sure it was heavy. After breakfast, we tried to move it. No luck. We did get it turned around and pointed toward the river, but could not move it closer to the water's edge. About an hour of struggle made it pretty clear that we were not going to push it the distance to the river.

Now we pondered what to do. Surely the dam would release more water and allow us to float away. But when? Luckily we had cell service, even if it was spotty. A few calls to some friends at the White River NWR confirmed that a major release of water was planned for later in the morning that should refloat our boat. All we had to do was wait. And wait we did, hour after hour, watching the river flow by with the only entertainment the occasional leap of an Asian flying carp plus my attempt to catch a largemouth bass. By early afternoon the water rise began and we watched in excitement as it slowly approached our stranded vessel. By now we had packed the boat with all our gear so all we would have to do was hop in and head down toward the Mississippi River as planned. After about two more hours the water was just touching the bow of the boat. We were eager to continue our trip, but all excitement faded at that moment as the water began to fall again. We tried in vain to push the boat into the water that was now much closer, but it was hopeless. By sundown the river was back down to the low level we had awoken to. I won't say what words were spoken, but suffice to say, there was vulgarity! The boat was unpacked, camp set up, and we prepared to spend our second night under the shadow of the great Yancopin Railroad Bridge.

November 12, 2011. Another spectacular cloudless night passed, and we awoke again to a chilly morning. More calls, now with worrisome draining batteries in our cell phones, provided no hope of extra water releases. We still had plenty of food and water, enough for several more days, but the time had come to surrender. We called 911!

The dispatcher on the other end of the line seemed slightly amused, although sympathetic enough. She said she would make some calls and see what she could do. I hoped that the small-town charm and friendliness Arkansas is known for would come through for us. Lo and behold it did. Around 2:00 p.m. our saviors arrived in the form of two four wheelers rumbling across the sand. It was the county sheriff, a park ranger, and two locals just willing to help out. Small-town Arkansas had come to our rescue, and I was pleased to think that life in the Delta was quiet enough for the sheriff to come all the way out here in a nonemergency to assist us.

Within minutes the four wheelers were attached to the boat, and we had it pulled back into the river. There were cheers all about, well, at least from Jenn and me. About this time, more folks arrived, this time two hunters on foot. Today had been the first day of modern gun season, and the deer hunters were out in force. Much to our surprise, the two hunters said that they had been in a deer stand just two hundred yards away, but unfortunately out of sight of us. Their deer camp with many more men was just a quarter mile away. They said they would have let us sleep in their warm cabin the previous night if they knew we were stuck down here and that we were welcome to stay with them now. They also mentioned, unnecessarily, that with all the men at the camp they probably could have gotten us back in to the water the previous day. We thanked them for their offer, but said we were anxious to get back home after our misadventure. Since we did not now have the time to make it down to the Mississippi, we turned back upstream to return to our starting point. Little did we know that our adventure was far from over.

The river was at least ten feet lower than when we began our downstream journey and what a difference that ten feet meant. Numerous obstructions, such as stumps and fallen logs, were present in many sections of the river and a real threat to the boat's propeller. We agreed that losing a prop now would not be fun, so it was slow going upstream. As we approached the last mile before the Pendleton Dam, we hit an extremely shallow section of river, less than a foot deep. In fact it was so shallow, we had to exit to the boat to reduce the weight and keep it off the bottom. So yes, now we were wading in ankle-deep water pushing the boat upstream. Fortunately both the water and the air were warm, so it was still worth a good laugh, especially considering our destination was almost in sight.

Finally, after four hours of upstream maneuvering we reached the boat ramp. What we saw there was not encouraging. It was a five-foot-high pile of sand where the ramp met the water. It had undoubtedly been deposited there during times of high water, but now was a major barrier to getting the boat out of the water. The irony was not lost on us. First we could not get the boat in the water, now we could not get it out! A couple of attempts with the truck and boat trailer confirmed that this was going to be difficult, mostly because my four-cylinder truck was not powerful enough to haul the boat and trailer over that great pile.

Once again though the kindness of Arkansans came to our rescue. Jenn walked up to main road and flagged down some hunters, now leaving the woods as the sun was setting. Their truck was also not powerful enough, but a couple of calls were made. The hunters told us that John was on his way and that although he "does have a lot of book smarts, he is not big on common sense." We did not know whether that was good or bad, but within minutes here came the monster truck. Although not normally a fan of the giant pickup, I was then. We had also begun to attract a crowd: another county sheriff, two Arkansas Game and Fish officers, an Army Corps of Engineer ranger, and five other random spectators who apparently had heard incorrectly that a boat had capsized. I said I was sorry to disappoint them, since I figured being blocked by a pile of sand was not as exciting as floating upside-down in the Arkansas. They said not to worry and that they would stay and watch anyway.

It was a struggle getting the boat from the river to the trailer, especially since we could not back the trailer all the way into the water. Without boring you further dear reader, let's just say with some muscle and some ill-advised use of the hand crank, we got it securely on the trailer. Unfortunately, one of our helpers broke his thumb doing it, which made me feel extremely bad, but he declined all help with medical costs and went on his way, presumably to the nearest hospital.

One thing we were sure of at this point. We were ready to leave and get home. The Arkansas Game and Fish Commission officers however were not. We were instead getting a thorough boat inspection. We passed with flying colors, although there was some debate about the fact that only I had a fishing license and there were two of us in the boat. I assured them (truthfully I might add) that Jenn does not fish. They seemed convinced and let us go on our way. I thanked them for their dedication to safety, and Jenn commended me on my attention to boat safety and Game and Fish regulations.

There was one final detail to complete before we got back on the road. The Army Corp ranger had been lobbying for some time from his superiors to get a backhoe assigned to Pendleton Dam because of the sand that kept blocking the aforementioned ramp. He said they had repeatedly declined his request. He then produced an incident document that he said would help. I signed it happily and wished him the best. He then asked if we were going to try our trip again in the future. I said maybe. He wished us luck.

It was thanks and goodnight to all our helpers and now our

adventure was truly over. It was a quick trip back to Arkansas City to get the car and then our two-vehicle caravan headed back home. Three hours and a long hot shower later, we sat down and had a stiff drink!

So what did I learn from this adventure and what wisdom can I pass on to you, future explorer of the Big Woods. First and foremost, we were reminded of the incredible hospitality and friendliness of the Arkansas people. There were so many that helped us out of our predicament, and they all did it out of the goodness of their heart (and some of them because it was their job, although I think they would have helped us anyway). Secondly, every Arkansas River explorer should look up the dam release schedule before going on the river. It is published online every day, for although the lands around the river are wild, the flow rates are still dictated by civilization. And thirdly, be careful out there. The Big Woods can be unforgiving. We were well prepared with food, water, and clothing, so were never in any real danger. The trip however was a reminder to remain prepared for the worst every time you enter the wilderness. If you decide to attempt this trip, do your homework and be prepared.

I have not tried that trip again, but I think I will someday. That wild stretch of the Arkansas River still calls me. Now I just have to convince Jenn to go with me again.

III FUTURE OF THE BIG WOODS

*"Conservation is a state of harmony
between men and land."*

—ALDO LEOPOLD, *Round River*

Several decades ago it appeared that all of the great bottomland forests of Arkansas's Mississippi Alluvial Plain would be gone. River channelization, levee construction, conversion to agriculture, and the appetite for wood were colluding to eliminate this great ecosystem. People took notice, though. The southern half of the White River NWR was already protected in 1935, but little else. The Cache River was at particular risk for many years as development interests lobbied for channelization projects that would irrevocably change the nature of the river. Indeed, the upper parts of the Cache River from the Missouri border to Newport were channelized, destroying the important headwaters. Channelization also occurred around the DeValls Bluff area, but work in this area was stopped by court order in 1973 (U.S. Army Corps of Engineers, 1973) and funding from Congress for the project became contentious thereafter.

Attitudes were also changing. Hunters, conservationists, and nature enthusiasts were concerned with the declines in wildlife, particularly waterfowl. The loss of forests and wetlands began to change public opinion as their value became more apparent when they became scarce. In 1952, land acquisition began on the Dagmar WMA, which preserved most of the old-growth swamp forest that remained in Arkansas. Wattensaw WMA was purchased from the US Forest Service in 1959 and protected an important area of upland forest, wetlands, and scattered grasslands. In 1971, the Black Swamp WMA was added to state holdings through several purchases. These three wildlife management area's protected very important habitats, but they remained physically isolated. Deforestation and wetland loss continued in the region.

Two major events help solidify and connect together the separate natural habitats. The authorization of the Cache River NWR in 1986 put a stop to the Cache River channelization project for good, and protected lands along the Cache from Clarendon to the small town of Grubbs, basically all of the Cache River that had not already been channelized. It also protected the lower sections of Bayou DeView from development (Lancaster, 2013). In 1993, a complex land swap and purchase allowed the White River NWR to buy lands between Clarendon and St. Charles and form what is now the North Unit of the refuge. This significant acquisition connected the southern and northern protected areas. Although land acquisition continues in the Cache River NWR and to a smaller extent in the White River NWR, a long stretch of protected land now extends about 125 miles. Extensive reforestation of lands along the Cache River, especially between the Black Swamp and the town of Clarendon, over time will connect widely separated forestland into a contiguous tract. Fortunately, trees are fast growing in the Big Woods, so it will not take that much time.

In 2013, the Cache River NWR and the White River NWR also proposed to extend their acquisition boundaries to include areas surrounding the current protected areas. If approved, the refuges will be allowed to buy land from willing landowners over a much larger area than currently allowed by law, which will connect additional habitat. This process will make the northern sections of the Big Woods much more contiguous, expand protection to the south around the Arkansas/White/ Mississippi River confluence, and will benefit those animals that require large ranges. The Nature Conservancy, in cooperation with the Army Corps of Engineers, is working to undo the damage done to the lower Cache River by channelization project of the 1970s, and will restore the river to its original course. As of 2015, phase one has been completed and water once again flows through much of the original channel.

Proper wildlife management has also improved the long-term prospects of many animals that inhabit the region. Waterfowl are actively managed (fig. 106), and duck hunting regulations are properly enforced today, so that most migratory duck species have very healthy populations. Black bears, once reduced to fewer than fifty individuals in the Big Woods, have rebounded to over five hundred, making their future much more secure, especially if expansion of protected land and reforestation is successful. They are carefully monitored in order to determine their population numbers and overall health (fig. 107)

So it could be argued that the future of Big Woods is bright. Big river-development projects appear to be a thing of the past as our modern society views conservation of natural resources as more important than continued development (at least sometimes). The Big Woods is now recognized as a globally significant wetland, and its magnificent wildlife is becoming better known to the public. In many ways, it is still

FIGURE 106: US Fish and Wildlife Service personnel banding wood ducks. Courtesy of Tabitha Holloway and the US Fish and Wildlife Service.

FIGURE 107: Fish and Wildlife Service personnel lowering a black bear cub from a den tree in order to collect biological measurements. Courtesy of Richard Hines and the US Fish and Wildlife Service.

an underutilized place. Except for the waterfowl hunters that descend upon it each winter, there is little use except by the local residents who know it well. But there are few places in the southern United States that can compete with its beauty and wildlife. I urge all to visit. Take a canoe trip, hike a trail, or fish one of the lakes, and I believe that you too will understand what makes the Big Woods such a special place.

Visitors' Information

LODGING, SUPPLIES, AND LOCAL ATTRACTIONS FROM NORTH TO SOUTH

An asterisk indicates a particularly enjoyable or interesting place to visit.*

Newport, AR

This moderate-sized town is located at the far north end of the Big Woods near the upper reaches of the Cache River. It has a wide variety of services available.

Smokehouse*: 601 Malcolm Avenue, Newport, AR, 72112; 870-217-0228. The sign is missing, but the large number of cars in the parking lot tells all. This is the local hang-out in Newport, and the barbecue and catfish dinners are excellent.

Fortune Inn & Suites: 901 Highway 367 N, Newport, AR, 72112; 870-523-5851.

Days Inn Newport: 101 Olivia Drive, Newport, AR, 72112; 870-523-6411.

Super Inn Newport: 1504 Highway 367 N, Newport, AR, 72112; 870-523-2768.

Augusta, AR

Augusta Motor Lodge: 220 Highway 64, Augusta, AR, 72006; 870-347-1055. Provides basic lodging.

Tamale Factory*: 19751 Highway 33 South, Augusta, AR, 72006; 870-347-1350. Not too surprisingly, they are known for their tamales but also for their steaks. It is actually located about ten miles south of Augusta in the tiny community of Gregory.

Cotija Mexican Restaurant: 5 Highway 64, Augusta, AR, 72006; 870-347-2233.

Des Arc, AR

This moderate-sized town located right on the White River is a few miles north of Interstate 40 and is conveniently located near the Wattensaw WMA and the Cache River NWR. It has an interesting history (including important Civil War history) and a moderate number of services.

Lower White River Museum State Park*: 2009 West Main Street, Des Arc, AR, 72040; 870-256-3711. This interesting museum houses exhibits on the Des Arc region, in particular the history of the White River industries. There is a particularly good explanation of the mussel industry and button making, which at one time was a major source of income in the Big Woods area.

Dondie's White River Princess Restaurant*: 101 East Curran Street, Des Arc, AR, 72040; 870-256-3311: Well-known establishment that looks like an old riverboat.

Brinkley, AR

This medium sized town on Interstate 40 just east of the Big Woods has grocery stores, gas stations, motels, and restaurants and is the best place for supplies in the vicinity of Interstate 40.

Motel 6: 2005 North Main Street, Brinkley, AR, 72021; 870-734-4680

Econo Lodge: 2203 North Main Street, Brinkley, AR, 72021; 870-734-1052

Days Inn: 1815 North Main Street, Brinkley, AR, 72021; 870-734-4300

Gene's Bar-B-Q: 1107 Arkansas 17, Brinkley, AR, 72021; 870-734-9965. They specialize in ribs.

Mom's Diner: Address: 1007 South Main, Brinkley, AR, 72021; 870-734-9923.

Paradise Hunting Lodge: Address: PO Box 531, Brinkley, AR, 72021; 870-734-2030. This lodge offers bird-watching tours in addition to their hunting excursions.

DeValls Bluff

This small town on the west bank of the White River just south of the Interstate 40 has a few basic services and also two famous eateries serving some southern classics. Several boat launches just off of Route 70 provide access to the White River within the Cache River NWR.

Ms. Lena's Fried Pies*: Intersection of Highway 33 at Highway 70, DeValls Bluff, AR, 72041; 870-998-7217. Ms. Lena's famous fried pies have attracted many fans over the years, including former president Bill Clinton. It is open only on Fridays and Saturdays.

Craig's Bar-B-Que*: 15 West Walnut, DeValls Bluff, AR, 72041; 870-998-2616. It doesn't look like much on the outside, but inside the pork sandwiches are to die for. I don't know what is in the barbecue sauce, and they are definitely not going to tell me, but it is by far the best in all of Arkansas.

White River Dairy Bar: 7759 Twin City Park Road, DeValls Bluff, AR, 72041; 870-998-7047. They are located just across the bridge on the east side of the White River and serve lunch and dinner Thursday through Saturday.

Hazen, AR

Just a few miles west of DeValls Bluff on Route 70, this small town has a few motels, services, and one really good restaurant.

Hurley House Cafe*: Intersection of Routes 63 and 70; 870-255-4679.Good local hangout known particularly for its breakfast. Lunch and dinner are fine too. If Ms. Lena's Fried Pies is closed, you can also buy fried pies here.

Clarendon, AR

This small town is located between the White River and Cache River NWRs and near the point where the two rivers merge. It has basic services and boat launch access to the White River.

J and M Motel: 321 S 5th Street, Clarendon, AR, 72029; 870-747-3322. Provides basic lodging.

Big Woods Birder's Lodge: 289 East Lake Lane, Holly Grove, AR, 72069; 501-590-5568. Offers lodging, guided nature tours, and hunting.

St. Charles, AR

St. Charles is located in the central section of the White River NWR and close to the visitor center within the refuge. It was once a strategic location on the White River during the Civil War, which makes for a fascinating history. A fair number of services are located in town and in the near vicinity.

Popa Duck Lodge*: 132 6th Street, PO Box 31, St. Charles, AR, 72140; 870-282-8888. This hunting lodge offers high-quality lodging and meals. It is usually full during duck season but often available at other times of the year: www.popaducklodge.com.

Maddox Bay Landing: 499 Resort Road, Holly Grove, AR, 72069; 870-462-8317 or 870-842-0533. Offers RV park, cabins, camping, bait shop, johnboat rental, supplies and five-dollar boat launch. Provides access to northern section of White River NWR. Maddox Bay (a lake) is known for good fishing.

Indian Bay: This small community is located on the east side of the White River Refuge just south of the Route 1 bridge over the White River. There is a public boat launch and primitive camping. A large Indian mound is visible just south of camping area.

Camper's Refuge: 2910 Highway 1, Saint Charles, AR, 72140; 870-282-3765. This facility has tent and RV camping available: http://www.campersrefuge.com.

St. Charles Museum★: 608 Broadway Street, St. Charles, AR, 72140. This charming little museum has good displays on the natural and cultural history of the region. It is a great place to stop on a rainy day.

Ethel, AR

It is just a few houses and a post office, but it is conveniently located near the Ethel entrance to the White River NWR.

Butler Lodge: 475 Bisswanger Road, Ethel, AR, 72048; 870-282-3283. This lodge provides convenient lodging and meals for those exploring the southern sections of the White River NWR.

Ethel Café★: Intersection of Route 17 and Ethel Road. Mary and Barbara run this really nice café that serves breakfast and lunch. It is quite the local hangout and is often packed with people during hunting season. The plate lunches are particularly good, and they make homemade pies every day. Basic outdoor supplies are also available for campers.

Mellwood, AR

Located in a remote section of the Big Woods, this tiny town is at the access road to the southeast corner of the White River NWR.

Mellwood Grocery*: 32299 Highway 44, Mellwood, AR, 72367; 870-827-6303. This is a classic country store with groceries, supplies, hardware, and many other items necessary for survival out in the country. It is the best place for supplies in this part of the Big Woods.

DeWitt, AR

This larger town in the southwestern area of the Big Woods has a good number of amenities including gas stations, convenience stores, a grocery, a few restaurants, and lodging.

Fowl Play Lodge: Duck Guides, Inc., PO Box 225, DeWitt, AR, 72042; 870-945-5511. This beautiful lodge is available outside of hunting season for larger groups. During duck season it is used exclusively by hunters: www.duck-guidesinc.com.

Bayou LaGrue Lodge: PO Box 592, DeWitt, AR, 72042; 870-946-5511. This lodge located near the White River NWR may have lodging available outside of hunting season.

Sahara Motel: 312 South Whitehead Drive, DeWitt, AR, 72042; 870- 946-3581. This motel provides basic accommodations.

Catfish Shack*: 306 South Whitehead Drive, DeWitt, AR, 72042; 870-946-8057. This restaurant has good fish dinners and appears to be a popular spot for the locals. The staff is invariably friendly, and it is my "go to" place in DeWitt.

Brunson's Honey Brown BBQ: 312 South Whitehead Drive, DeWitt, AR, 72042; 870-946-2641.

Gillett, AR

This small town in the southwestern edge of Big Woods has a few limited services.

> **Arkansas Post State Park:** 5530 Highway 165 South, Gillett, AR, 72055; 870-548-2634. Located just a few miles south of Gillett, this park has displays of typical settler houses from the late 1800s.

> **Rice Paddy Motel and Restaurant:** 4379 Highway 165 S, Gillett, AR, 72055.

Pendleton, AR

Pendleton is a small unincorporated community situated around the Pendleton Dam in the far south of the Big Woods. Large Corps of Engineer's campgrounds are located here, but not many services. The area is popular with fisherman.

> **Casa del Rio Motel and Pendleton Sandbar Restaurant:** 170 Pendleton Lane, Dumas, AR, 71639; 870-382-8990. This establishment is located just downstream from the bridge over the Arkansas River.

> **Wilbur D. Mills Park:** This large, modern campground is located just downstream of the Pendleton Dam. It has a boat launch into the river, restrooms, and RV hookups.

> **Pendleton Bend Park:** Another large campground with the same amenities as the Wilbur D. Mills Park, but it is located just upstream from the Pendleton Dam.

Dumas, AR

Larger town in the southwest area of the Big Woods. It is a bit far from most of the good wildlife areas, but it has a good supply of services including a few chain motels that will provide satisfactory and predictable, if unspectacular lodging. Several attractions in town and nearby areas should not be missed. If you have a rainy day, Dumas and its vicinity is a good place to spend some time.

Dumas Inn: 722 Highway 65 South, Dumas, AR, 71639; 877-233-4885.

Executive Inn: 310 Highway 65 South, Dumas, AR; 870-382-5115.

Days Inn: 501 Highway 65 South, Dumas, AR, 71639; 888-330-0175.

Miller's Mud Mill★: Highway 65 South, Brookhaven Shopping Center, Dumas, AR 71639; 870-382-5277. Gail Miller and her staff run this fascinating shop with high-quality pottery that has been featured in publications across the country. Stop in and they will delight in telling you about their work. Their shop is in a shopping center on the south end of town.

Taylor's Restaurant★: 14201 Highway 54, Dumas, AR, 71639; 870-382-5349. Located just west of Dumas on Route 54, it was once a grocery. It has been remodeled into a restaurant and now serves high-end dinners, in particular steaks. You can see the aging beef cuts on display through the glass in the freezers. The steaks are some of the best served anywhere in Arkansas.

R. A. Pickens and Son Company★: 122 Pickens Road, Pickens, AR, 71662; 870-382-5266. This is one not to miss! It is a combination restaurant, general store, post office, and office for the large farm. The food is plentiful and delicious, while the atmosphere seems lost in another time. The country-style meals and amazing desserts will make you happy, but you will have to walk or canoe many miles to work off the calories.

Rohwer, AR

This very small town about thirty miles south of the Big Woods has an important historical site.

Rohwer Japanese Relocation Center*: WWII Japanese-American Internment Museum, 100 South Railroad Street, PO Box 1263, McGehee, AR, 71654 (please note that this address is the mailing address. Visit the website http://rohwer.astate.edu/ for directions to the site); 870-222-9168.

This National Historic Site preserves part of what could more properly be called a concentration camp and represents one of the most shameful chapters in American history. During World War II, thousands of American citizens of Japanese descent, mostly from California, were forcibly removed from their homes, stripped of their property, and moved to various parts of the United States, including this camp in southeastern Arkansas. They were considered potential enemies of the state, and government officials worried that some might be spies for Japan. Remarkably, the Supreme Court upheld their imprisonment, which lasted the duration of the war. Many died here and are interred in the small cemetery. A large stone monument commemorates the Japanese American soldiers from this camp killed in action in Europe, volunteers who served their country while their families remained imprisoned. Their company was the most decorated of any in the European Theater. After the war, all of these citizens were released, although many never regained their property. No Japanese American anywhere in the United States was ever charged with a war-related crime. The site has recently been upgraded to enhance the visitor experience. George Takei, Mr. Sulu of Star Trek fame, spent some of his childhood here and has visited in recent years.

CANOE AND KAYAK RENTALS
AND GUIDED TOURS OF THE REGION

Quapaw Canoe Company

291 Sunflower Avenue, Clarksdale, MS, 38614; 662-627-4070 or 870-228-2266. This company, although located in Mississippi, offers guided tours of Big Woods' rivers and streams, including trips down the Mississippi River. Call for availability.

Canoeman River Guide Services

616 South Colorado Street Celina, TX, 75009; 214-998-4922. Although located in Texas, this company does occasional trips to the Big Woods.

Internet Resources

Arkansas Game and Fish Commission: http://www.agfc.com/

Sheffield Nelson Dagmar WMA: http://www.agfc.com/hunting/Pages/wmaDetails.aspx?show=575

Mike Freeze Wattensaw WMA: http://www.agfc.com/hunting/Pages/wmadetails.aspx?show=433

Rex Hancock Black Swamp WMA: http://www.agfc.com/hunting/Pages/wmaDetails.aspx?show=550

Trusten Holder WMA: http://www.agfc.com/hunting/Pages/wmaDetails.aspx?show=630

Watchable Wildlife Program http://www.agfc.com/species/Pages/SpeciesWatchableWildlife.aspx#3

Arkansas Natural Heritage Commission: http://www.naturalheritage.com/

Arkansas State Parks: http://www.arkansasstateparks.com/

Arkansas Post National Memorial: http://www.nps.gov/arpo/index.htm

Cache River at Patterson: http://waterdata.usgs.gov/ar/nwis/uv/?site_no=07077500&PARAmeter_cd=00065,00060

Cache River NWR: http://www.fws.gov/cacheriver/

The Nature Conservancy: Big Woods Link: http://www.nature.org/ourinitiatives/regions/northamerica/unitedstates/arkansas/ivorybill/big-woods-of-arkansas.xml

USGS Bayou DeView water gauge: http://waterdata.usgs.gov/usa/nwis/uv?07077730

USGS White River water gauge at DeValls Bluff: http://waterdata.usgs.gov/ar/nwis/uv/?site_no=07077000&PARAmeter_cd=00065,00060

White River NWR: http://www.fws.gov/whiteriver/

Local and Federal Officials

White County Sheriff: 501-279-6279 (Northern Cache River NWR, Black Swamp WMA vicinity)

Woodruff County Sheriff: 870-347-2583 (Central Cache River NWR, Dagmar MWA vicinity)

Prairie County Sheriff: 870-256-4137 (Southern Cache River NWR, Wattensaw WMA vicinity)

Monroe County Sheriff: 870-747-3811 (Dagmar WMA, Northern White River NWR vicinity)

Arkansas County Sheriff: 870-673-2121 (White River NWR, Trusten Holder WMA vicinity)

Desha County Sheriff: 870-877-2327 (Southern White River NWR, Trusten Holder WMA vicinity)

Cache River NWR: 870-347-2614

Rex Hancock Black Swamp WMA: 877-734-4581

Sheffield Nelson Dagmar WMA: 877-734-4581

Mike Freeze Wattensaw WMA: 877-734-4581

White River NWR: 870-282-8200

Trusten Holder WMA: 877-367-3559

Arkansas Post NM: 870-548-2207

For all emergencies dial 911

Checklist of Sites

_____ 1. Cache River Canoe Trail

_____ 2. Black Swamp Hiking Trail

_____ 3. Black Swamp Canoe Trail

_____ 4. Bayou DeView Swamp Canoe Trail

_____ 5. Bayou DeView Birding Water Trail

_____ 6. Birding Trail at Apple Lake

_____ 7. Mud Slough Birding Trail

_____ 8. Robe Bayou Canoe Trail

_____ 9. Wattensaw Bayou Water Trail

_____ 10. Hurricane Creek Hiking Trail

_____ 11. Lambert Bayou/Swan Lake Float

_____ 12. Moon Lake Canoe Trail

_____ 13. Bottomland Hardwood Trail

_____ 14. Upland Trail

_____ 15. CCC Trail

_____ 16. Observation Tower Trail

_____ 17. Big Island Chute Trail

_____ 18. Big Horseshoe Lake Hiking Trail

_____ 19. Big Cypress Tree Trail

_____ 20. H-Lake Canoe Loop

_____ 21. East Moon Lake/Parish Lakes Float

_____ 22. Sugarberry Natural Area

_____ 23. Post Bayou Nature Trail

_____ 24. Arkansas River Nature Trail

_____ 25. Arkansas Post Water Trail

_____ 26. Handicapped Accessible Hiking Trail

_____ 27. LaGrues Lake Hiking Trail

_____ 28. Pine City Natural Area/Red-Cockaded Woodpecker Site

_____ 29. Louisiana Purchase Historic State Park

_____ 30. Railroad Prairie and Downs Prairie Natural Areas

REFERENCES

Arkansas Natural Heritage Commission. 2013. The Grand Prairie of Arkansas, Past, Present, and Future. 2nd Edition.

Arkansas Soil and Water Conservation Commission. 1988. Arkansas State Water Plan: Eastern Arkansas Basin. Little Rock, AR.

Biedenharn, D. S., C. R. Thorne, and C. C. Watson. 2000. Recent morphological evolution of the Lower Mississippi River. Geomorphology. 34(3-4): 227–249.

Bird Life International. 2012. *Euphagus carolinus*. In: IUCN 2013. IUCN Red List of Threatened Species. Version 2013.1

Blehert, D. S., A. C. Hicks, M. Behr, C. U. Meteyer, B. M. Berlowski-Zier, E. L. Buckles, J. T. H. Coleman, S. R. Darling, A. Gargas, R. Niver, J. C. Okoniewski, R. J. Rudd, and W. B. Stone. 2009. Bat white-nose syndrome: An emerging fungal pathogen? Science 323:227.

Blockstein, D. E. 1998. Lyme disease and the passenger pigeon? Science 279:1831.

Bour, R. 2007. Global diversity of turtles (Chelonii; Reptilia) in freshwater. Hydrobiologia 595:593–598.

Bragg, D. C. 2005. Presettlement *Pinus taeda* in the Mississippi Valley Alluvial Plain of the Monroe County, Arkansas area. Journal of the Arkansas Academy of Sciences. 59:187–195.

Briand, C. H. 2000. Cypress knees: An enduring enigma. Arnoldia. 60:19–20, 21–25.

Bryant, M. D. 2010. Past and present aquatic habitats and fish populations of the Yazoo-Mississippi Delta. Gen. Tech. Rep. SRS-130. Asheville, NC: U.S. Department of Agriculture Forest Service, Southern Research Station.

Christian, A. A., J. L. Harris, W. R. Posey, J. F. Hockmuth, and G. L. Harp. 2005. Freshwater mussel (Bivalvia: Unionidae) assemblages of the Lower Cache River, Arkansas. Southeastern Naturalist 4:487–512.

Clark, D. W., S. C. White, A. K. Bowers, L. D Lucio, and G. A. Heidt. 2002. A survey of recent accounts of the mountain lion (*Puma concolor*) in Arkansas. Southeastern Naturalist 1:269-278.

Cokinos, C. 2009. Hope Is a Thing with Feathers. Tarcher Press, New York, NY.

Collins, J. T., R. Conant, R. T. Peterson, I. H. Conant, and T. R. Johnson. 1998. A Field Guide to Reptiles and Amphibians: Eastern and Central North America (Peterson Field Guides). Houghton Mifflin Harcourt, Boston, MA.

Collinson, J. Martin. 2007. Video analysis of the escape flight of pileated woodpecker *Dryocopus pileatus*: Does the ivory-billed woodpecker *Campephilus principalis* persist in continental North America? BMC Biology 5:8.

Csiki, I., C. Lam, A. Key, E. Coulter, J. D. Clark, R. M. Pace, K. G. Smith, and D. D. Rhoads. 2003. Genetic variation in black bears in Arkansas and Louisiana using microsatellite DNA markers. Journal of Mammalogy 84:691–701.

Delnicke, D., and K. J. Reinecke. 1986. Mid-winter food use and body weights of mallards and wood ducks in Mississippi. Journal of Wildlife Management 50:43–51.

DeLorme Atlas and Gazetteer Series. 2011. Arkansas Atlas and Gazetteer. DeLorme Publishing, Yarmouth, ME.

Eggleton, M. A., and H. L. Schramm. 2004. Feeding ecology and energetic relationships with habitat of blue catfish, *Ictalurus furcatus*, and flathead catfish, *Pylodictis olivaris*, in the Lower Mississippi River, U.S.A. Environmental Biology of Fishes 70:107–121.

Ellsworth, J. W., and B. C. McComb. 2003. Potential effects of passenger pigeon flocks on the structure and composition of presettlement forests of eastern North America. Conservation Biology 17: 1548–1558.

Ernst, C. H., J. E. Lovich, and R. W. Barbour. 1994. Turtles of the United States and Canada. Smithsonian Institution Press, Washington, DC.

Ernst, T. 2006. Arkansas Nature Lover's Guidebook. Cloudland.net Publishing, Pettigrew, AR.

Fitzpatrick, J. W., M. Lammertink, M. D. Luneau, T. W. Gallagher, B. R. Harrison, G. M. Sparling, K. V. Rosenberg, R. W. Rohrbaugh, E. C. H. Swarthout, P. H. Wrege, S. B. Swarthout, M. S. Dantzker, R. A. Charif, T. R. Barksdale, J. V. Remsen, S. D. Simon, and D. Zollner. 2005. Ivory-billed woodpecker (*Campephilus principalis*) persists in continental North America. Science 308:1460–1462.

Futuyma, D. J., and F. Gould. 1979. Associations of plants and insects in deciduous forest. Ecological Monographs 49:33–50.

Harris, J. L., and M. E. Gordon. 1990. Arkansas Mussels. Arkansas Game and Fish Commission, Little Rock, AR.

Haag, W. R. 2012. North American Freshwater Mussels: Natural History, Ecology, and Conservation. Cambridge University Press, Cambridge, UK.

Hoekstra, J., J. L. Molnar, M. Jennings, C. Revenga, M. D. Spalding, and K. Ellison. 2010. The Atlas of Global Conservation: Changes, Challenges, and Opportunities to Make a Difference. University of California Press, Berkeley, CA.

Hunter, C. G. 2000. Wildflowers of Arkansas. Ozark Society Foundation, Fayetteville, AR.

Hunter, C. G. 2000. Trees, Shrubs, and Vines of Arkansas. Ozark Society Foundation, Fayetteville, AR.

Keeler, Harriet L. 1900. Our Native Trees and How to Identify Them. Charles Scriber's Sons, New York, NY.

Kelly, D., Koenig, W. D., and A. M. Leibhold. 2008. An intercontinental comparison of the dynamic behavior of mast seeding communities. Population Ecology 50:329–342.

Kennedy, H. E. 2009. Sugarberry. Encyclopedia of Life.

Key, J. P. 2012. European Exploration and Settlement, 1541 through 1802. Encyclopedia of Arkansas.

Krammerer, J. C. 1990. Largest Rivers in the United States. United States Geological Survey, Department of Interior.

Krementz, D. G., and J. D. Lusier. 2010. Woodpecker densities in the Big Woods of Arkansas. Journal of Fish and Wildlife Management. 1:102–110.

Krochmal, A. R., G. S. Bakken, and T. J. LaDuc. 2007. Heat in evolution's kitchen: Evolutionary perspectives on the functions and origin of the facial pit of pit vipers (Viperidae: Crotalinae). Journal of Experimental Biology 207:4231–4238.

Lancaster, G. 2013. Cache River. Encyclopedia of Arkansas.

Larson, Lee W. 1996. The Great USA Flood of 1993. International Association of Hydrological Sciences Conference: Destructive water: Water-caused natural disasters—Their abatement and control.

Müller-Schwarze, D., and L. Sun. 2003. The Beaver: Natural History of a Wetlands Engineer. Cornell University Press, Ithaca, NY.

Nelson, J. C. 1997. Presettlement vegetation patterns along the 5th principal meridian, Missouri Territory, 1815. American Midland Naturalist 137:79–94.

Nelson, J. S. 2006. Fishes of the World. John Wiley & Sons, Inc., Hoboken, NJ.

Nuttall, T. 1819. A Journal of Travels into the Arkansas Territory During the Year 1819, ed. Savioe Lottinville. Reprint ed. 1999. University of Arkansas Press, Fayetteville, AR.

Oli, M.D., H.A. Jacobson, and B.D. Leopold. 1997. Denning ecology of black bears in the White River National Wildlife Refuge, Arkansas. Journal of Wildlife Management 61:700–706.

Odegaard, F. 2000. How many species of arthropods? Erwin's estimate revised. Biological Journal of the Linnean Society 71:583–597.

Paxton, J. R., and W. N. Eschmeyer. 1998. Encyclopedia of Fishes. Academic Press, San Diego, CA.

Penfound, W. T., and T. T. Earle. 1948. The biology of the water hyacinth. Ecological Monographs 18:447–472.

Reimer, R. D. 1963. The crawfish of Arkansas. M.S. Thesis, University of Arkansas, Fayetteville, AR.

Ricciardi, A., and J. B. Rasmussen. 1999. Extinction rates of North American freshwater fauna. Conservation Biology 13:1220–1222.

Rosell, F., O. Bozser, P. Collen, and H. Parker. 2005. Ecological impact of beavers, *Castor canadensis* and their ability to modify ecosystems. Mammal Review 35:248–276.

Rosen, R. A., and D. C. Hales. 1981. Feeding of paddlefish, *Polyodon spathula*. Copeia 2:441–455.

Rupar, B., and M. D. Warriner. 2009. Arkansas's Lost Pines. Arkansas Natural Heritage Commission.

Sibley, D. A. 2000. The Sibley Guide to Birds. Alfred A. Knopf Publishing, New York, NY.

Sibley, D. A., L. R. Bevier, M. A. Patten, and C. S. Elphick. 2006. Comment on "Ivory-billed woodpecker (*Campephilus principalis*) persists in continental North America." Science 311:1555.

Smith, G. R., C. Badgley, T. P. Eiting, and P. S. Larson. 2010. Species diversity gradients in relation to geological history in North American freshwater fishes. Evolutionary Ecology Research 12: 693–726.

Spond, M. D. 2007. Ancient cypress-tupelo forest at the Dagmar Wildlife Management Area. M.A. Thesis, University of Arkansas, Fayetteville, AR.

Sutton, K. B. 1998. Arkansas Wildlife: A History. University of Arkansas Press, Fayetteville, AR.

Sutton, K. B. 2013. Gars and Arrows: Pursuit Has storied History, Uncertain Fate. Arkansas Online. Arkansas Democrat-Gazette.

Tanner, James T. 1942. The Ivory-Billed Woodpecker. National Audubon Society, New York, NY.

Taylor, C. A., M. L. Warren Jr., J. F. Fitzpatrick, H. H. Hobbs, R. F. Jezerinac, W. L. Pflieger, and H. W. Robison. 1996. Conservation status of the crayfishes of the U.S. and Canada. Fisheries. 22:25–38.

Turgeon, D. D., A. E. Bogan, E. V. Coan, W. K., Emerson, W. G. Lyons, W. L. Pratt, C. F. E. Roper, A. Scheltema, F. G. Thompson, and J. D. Williams. 1988. Common and Scientific Names of Aquatic Invertebrates from the United States and Canada: Mollusks. American Fisheries Society Special Publication 16, Bethesda, Maryland. 277 pp.

U.S. Army Corps of Engineers. 1973. Draft Environmental Impact Statement Cache River Basin Project, Arkansas. U.S. Army Corps of Engineers, Memphis District.

U.S. Department of Agriculture, Forest Service. 1965. Silvics of forest trees of the United States. H. A. Fowells, comp. U.S. Department of Agriculture, Agriculture Handbook 271. Washington, DC.

U.S. Forest and Wildlife Service. 1994. Comprehensive Management Plan for the Cache River and White River National Wildlife Refuges, within the Cache/Lower White Rivers Ecosystem. U.S. Department of the Interior, Fish and Wildlife Service.

U.S. Forest and Wildlife Service. 2008. American Alligator *Alligator mississippiensis*. U.S. Department of the Interior, Fish and Wildlife Service.

U.S. Forest and Wildlife Service. 2007. Red Wolf (*Canis rufus*) 5-Year Status Review: Summary and Evaluation. U.S. Department of the Interior, Fish and Wildlife Service.

U.S. Forest and Wildlife Service. 2012. White River National Wildlife Refuge. Draft Comprehensive Conservation Plan and Environmental Assessment. U.S. Department of the Interior, Fish and Wildlife Service.

Unterberger, Richie. 1997. Treasury of Library of Congress Field Recordings—Various Artists : Songs, Reviews, Credits, Awards. AllMusic.

Walters, J. R., P. D. Doerr, and J. H. Carter. 1988. The cooperative breeding system of the red-cockaded woodpecker. Ethology, 78: 275–305.

Walters, J. R. 1991. Application of ecological principles to the management of endangered species: The case of the red-cockaded woodpecker. Annual Review of Ecology and Systematics 22:505–523.

Woods A. J., T. L. Foti, S. S. Chapman, J. M. Omernik, J. A. Wise, E. O. Murray, W. L. Prior, J. B. Pagan, Jr., J. A. Comstock, and M. Radford. 2004. Ecoregions of Arkansas (color poster with map, descriptive text, summary tables, and photographs). U.S. Geological Survey Reston, VA. map scale 1:1,000,000.

Wright, J. P., C. G. Jones, and A. S. Flecker. 2002. An ecosystem engineer, the beaver, increases species richness at the landscape scale. Oecologia 132:96–101.